IN SEARCH OF SOUTHERN EUROPE

IN SEARCH

OF

SOUTHERN

EUROPE

Reader's
Digest

PUBLISHED BY THE READER'S DIGEST ASSOCIATION LIMITED

LONDON   NEW YORK   MONTREAL   SYDNEY   CAPE TOWN

Originally published in partwork form,
Des Pays et des Hommes,
by Librairie Larousse, Paris

A Reader's Digest selection

IN SEARCH OF SOUTHERN EUROPE

First English Edition Copyright © 1992
The Reader's Digest Association Limited, Berkeley Square House,
Berkeley Square, London W1X 6AB

Copyright © 1992
Reader's Digest Association Far East Limited
Philippines Copyright 1992
Reader's Digest Association Far East Limited

Originally published in French as a partwork,
Des Pays et des Hommes
Copyright © 1983, 1985
Librairie Larousse

Translated and edited by Toucan Books Limited, London
Translated and adapted by Andrew Kerr-Jarrett and Alex Martin

ISBN 0 276 42051 9

Printed by Printer Industria Gráfica S.A., Barcelona

Contents

COVER PICTURES

Top: *From the Esplanade in Corfu Town, there are magnificent views of the fortress, perched on a promontory and dating from the 16th century. The coast of mainland Greece shimmers in the background.*

Bottom: *A pair of oxen pull a cart across the Tuscan countryside: a scene that has hardly changed in hundreds of years.*

The Crucible of Western Civilisation

For the ancient Romans, the Mediterranean was the centre of the Earth, the Great Sea or *Mare Magnum* that lay at the heart of their maps of the known world. For countless men and women ever since, two of the lands that line its northern shores have remained the heart of the civilised world, places of a special enchantment whose magic lies in the blending of a glorious and overwhelming cultural heritage with the beauty of their landscapes, their patterns of life, their foods and wines. Here, in ancient Greece and Rome, the Western traditions of art, philosophy, politics, literature and drama had their birth. Centuries later, in the Renaissance, Italy gave rise to most of the period's finest works of art, architecture and literature. Later again, the focus of interest widened to include the Atlantic coast, as the Portuguese and Spanish embarked on the extraordinary adventures of navigation that led them around Africa to the fabled lands of the Orient and across the Atlantic to the Americas.

Witnesses to the great days abound: in the stately white columns of ruined temples in Greece (most famously the Parthenon in Athens); in Italian hilltop towns that seem to have emerged, barely changed, from the background detail of some early Renaissance painting of the Virgin and Child; in the ornately embellished Spanish and Portuguese palaces, churches and convents built on the wealth of the Indies and the Americas.

But if the lands of Southern Europe can justly claim to be the 'cradle' of Western civilisation, they have also witnessed some rather grimmer events. In the 20th century, Spain and the various republics of what used to be the federal Yugoslav state have been riven by cruel and bloody civil wars. The Spanish Civil War, seen by many historians as a kind of rehearsal for the Second World War, left a million people dead or forced into exile and saw outstanding atrocities such as the bombing of Guernica in the north – this was made famous by Picasso's horrified reaction to it and his painting of the same name. Symbolic of the wanton destructiveness of the later Yugoslav conflict was the wrecking of large areas of Dubrovnik, one of the finest architectural gems of the whole Mediterranean, during massive bombardments in 1991. On top of these brutal records, the 20th century has also seen the desecration of large expanses of the northern Mediterranean's beautiful coastline, all in the name of tourism (admittedly, an economic lifeline for many of the poorer parts of the region), not to mention an ever-rising level of pollution in a sea with scarcely any tides and just one tiny inlet to the Atlantic through the Strait of Gibraltar.

For all that, the appeal of Southern Europe remains unchanged. Few regions of the world have given birth to such an astonishing succession of civilisations, and few can boast such a concentration of monuments: from the Palace of Knossos in Crete (dating from between the 17th and 15th centuries BC when the local Minoan civilisation was at its height) to the Colosseum in Rome; from Florence's Renaissance *Duomo* (Cathedral) to Barcelona's extraordinary monument to *modernismo*, the Church of the Sagrada Familia. Entire cities stand as emblems of past glories: most notably Venice which throughout the Middle Ages and afterwards ruled a large maritime empire in the Mediterranean (the city is now under threat as it sinks gently into the very lagoon that in its days of wealth provided its defence).

These empires and civilisations did not, however, go unchallenged in their domination of the region. At its greatest extent the Venetian Empire reached far into the eastern Mediterranean, but it had to retract in the face of the expanding might of the Muslim Ottoman Empire. The Ottomans had captured Byzantium (modern Istanbul), capital of the eastern sector of the Roman Empire, in 1453 and went on to swallow up Greece (which only regained its freedom in the early 19th century) and large parts of the Adriatic coast. The effects of this division of Southern Europe are still with us: the battling Serbs and Croats of Yugoslavia, for example, have the same ethnic roots and speak virtually the same language – but a major difference between them is that the Serbs spent centuries within the orbit of Byzantium and the Ottoman Empire, while the Croats were always more closely aligned with the West.

The Iberian peninsula, meanwhile, also fell under Muslim rule. In AD 711, Tariq ibn Ziyad, the Muslim Governor of Tangier, crossed the Strait of Gibraltar and defeated the last of Spain's Visigothic rulers, King Roderick. The Moors soon had the whole peninsula at their feet and were to remain there for just under eight centuries – only in 1492 was the slow process of the *Reconquista* completed. The Christian Spanish and Portuguese finally regained control of their lands when Granada surrendered to the Catholic monarchs, Ferdinand and Isabella. For their part, the Moors were enlightened rulers who tolerated Christians and Jews as well as Muslims and presided over a flowering of the arts and sciences. Numerous memorials to their skills survive, from the tessellated glories of the Alhambra palace in Granada to the irrigation channels that still provide the vital water for the fertile but dry soils around Valencia in eastern Spain.

In part, at least, this mingling of influences accounts for the striking vitality of Southern Europe's culture. Certainly, the region has from the very earliest times thrown up outstanding artists, writers and thinkers: three of the most influential poets of all time, from the Greek Homer in the 9th or 8th century BC, to the Roman Virgil and the Florentine Dante; the three giants of high Renaissance art, Michelangelo, Leonardo da Vinci and Raphael; the 16th-century Spaniard Cervantes, creator of Don Quixote; composers such as the Italian Verdi; and in the vanguard of the 20th-century modernist movement, the Spaniards Picasso and Salvador Dalí. But the achievements of Southern European culture are not confined to the high arts. The people of the region can also boast thriving popular arts and traditions. Festivals abound, from the spectacular bull-runnings of Pamplona's *Sanfermines* to the various *panighiri* (festivals in honour of local patron saints) and *apokries* (pre-Lenten carnivals) in Greece, and they are all enjoyed for their own sake, not just as tourist attractions. Playing an essential part in most of them are folk traditions of music, singing and dancing, and here again the diversity is enormous – from the melancholy strains of Portuguese *fado* to the hypnotic rhythms of Spanish *flamenco* to the intoxicating patterns of the *pentozalis* dance from eastern Crete. The demands of modern life mean that national costumes have long disappeared in most places, except for folklore displays and the like. Even so, there are parts of Serbia where the women still don their traditional garments of white with gold-coloured embroidery to gather in the harvest in autumn.

Modern times have, of course, brought enormous changes throughout the region. Electricity and the motor vehicle have spread into even the remotest villages. Televisions blare out from bars; the smallest towns have their discotheques where young people girate to the sounds of British or American rock and pop. Nor is Southern Europe any longer an economic or political backwater lagging behind its more dynamic neighbours to the north. Governments may come and go with bewildering rapidity in Rome, but the economy of northern Italy, in particular, has boomed since the Second World War, with the country as a whole joining the ranks of the seven richest nations on Earth. During the 1970s, Greece, Portugal and Spain each threw off dictatorial regimes and embraced democracy – and each in due course joined the European Community. Joining the European mainstream did not bring immediate prosperity to Greece or Portugal, but the dramatic success of the Spanish economy in the late 1980s and early 90s was an inspiring example – it also sent the employees of numerous multinational companies scuttling to brush up their knowledge of the language, the better to exploit the opportunities opening up there.

All of this has accentuated regional differences that have long existed: between the rich, industrial north of Italy and the still relatively impoverished south, for example; between Milan with its international reputation for design and engineering and Naples with its virtually Third World levels of poverty and high crime rate; between Catalonia with its long traditions of commercial and industrial success and the stark lands of Extremadura in west-central Spain; between the Alpine orderliness and efficiency of Slovenia and the more feudal way of life of Montenegro. And yet, even in the most prosperous areas, you are still constantly confronted with images to remind you that the past has endured into the present. Unsightly concrete hotels may spread along much of the coastline, but inland and in less exploited coastal areas, the villages still sparkle blindingly white under the blue sky and brilliant sun. Vines and olive trees cast their shade across the slopes, while the wheat from flatter lands still goes into a multitude of crusty local breads. Old women in black shelter from the midday heat on their doorsteps, and when dusk comes the men still foregather in the bars of main squares. Modern housing blocks and industrial estates may have sprouted around the towns and cities, but at their centres the narrow, musty streets of Gothic quarters cluster around soaring cathedrals, and the imposing fronts of baroque palaces and churches still look down on their squares. War, poverty and pollution have all wrought their havoc at various times over the centuries, but the lands of Southern Europe are still able to cast their spell of enchantment.

Spain

Few European countries can boast more variety than Spain. From the green mountains of Galicia, to the stark lands of the high Castilian plateau, to the near deserts of eastern Andalucía, it encompasses a huge range of landscapes and cultures. Although long isolated behind the mountain barrier of the Pyrenees and by the vagaries of its politics, Spain is now a thriving democracy, rediscovering its place in the European mainstream. Even so, it still clings to the traditions and colourful festivals that are a heritage of the many races who have left their mark on its life – from Phoenicians to Visigoths, Romans to Moors.

Basque fishermen's children
lend a hand in mending their
fathers' nets. The local
seafaring tradition has long
roots. In the 14th century, the
Basques were hunting whales
off the Greenland coast, and
in the 16th century they
crewed many of the ships that
took the Spanish discoverers
to the New World.

Previous page:
The coal-black hat and jacket
are part of the traditional
costume of the Andalucian
landowner.

Sitges, south of Barcelona on
the Costa Dorada, is one of
the prettier and less spoiled of
Catalonia's seaside resorts.
At weekends in the summer,
it is popular with young
Barcelonans who like to
wander through its narrow
streets and enjoy the seafood
in its restaurants.

Green Lands of Northern Spain

Every Sunday morning, men and women of all ages and types gather in the main squares of the cities, towns and villages of Spain's north-east region of Catalonia. They take off their shoes, replacing them with rope-soled *espardenyes* (espadrilles), make a heap of their belongings and gravely link hands to form a circle – man, woman, man, woman and so on. A group of musicians then strikes up on the *flaviol* (a small flute), *tenora* (a kind of oboe) and drum, and an age-old ritual begins: the *Sardana,* Catalonia's traditional dance.

With the musicians setting a repetitive, mesmerising, triple-time rhythm, the dancers embark on a series of complicated movements, surging inwards with strange, bounding steps and pacing sideways. The dancing gathers pace. The beat of the music becomes ever more insistent, and the dancers have to stay constantly alert to keep in time. After a while, latecomers join in, until in some cases the circle (*colla*) becomes so large that it splits into two smaller ones, which may in turn grow and split. Eventually, in the larger cities such as Barcelona, the entire square is a mass of figures moving and surging to the beat of the music; the whole spectacle has something of the hypnotic quality of sea waves breaking on a rock.

It is all very different from the flamboyant, foot-tapping patterns of the more famous dances of southern Spain, and its stately rhythms speak loudly of the traditions that distinguish Catalonia from the rest of Spain. In its present form, the *Sardana* originated in the district of La Cerdaña in the Catalan Pyrenees, but it is in fact a relic of pre-Christian fertility rites once common throughout the Mediterranean. Its various phases represent the calm of the night, the first cock crow, the eventual triumph of the sun and the dawn chorus of birds. The Minoans of ancient Crete depicted a similar dance on their pots, and Homer describes one that figured on Achilles's shield. To the modern Catalans, the *Sardana* is a kind of anthem, an expression of their nationhood.

A proud nation

Catalonia (Catalunya to the Catalans, and Cataluña to other Spanish people) is very much a nation, quite different from the rest of Spain – as the Catalans themselves are invariably the first to point out. Simply crossing the frontier from southern France is enough to prove it. To the north lies French Languedoc-Roussillon, to the south the Catalan plain of Empordà. Despite the great mountain barrier of the Pyrenees slicing between them, both regions clearly belong to one community – one nation, the more ardent local nationalists will tell you. Admittedly, a few of the crops are different: on the French side, neat rows of vegetables, tomatoes, apricots and other fruits; on the

drier Catalan side, the classic Mediterranean trilogy of wheat, vines and olive trees, with a few almonds and carobs. But the basics of the landscape are the same. And if geography is not enough, the names themselves offer hints. Languedoc unravels as Langue d'Oc, the distinctive language of large parts of southern France, virtually identical to the language of Catalonia. It is these ties of geography and culture linking the Catalans as much with places outside the frontiers of Spain, as with those within, that mark them out so clearly from the rest of their countrymen.

Catalonia is not one of those Mediterranean lands consisting largely of wide coastal plains. A few fertile plains have formed around the deltas of rivers such as the Llobregat near Barcelona. Elsewhere, mountain ranges, dominated by the serrated, 4000-foot profile of

The Catalans, like the Basques, have their fishing and seafaring traditions. In the Middle Ages, they were one of the Mediterranean's great trading powers, whose influence reached as far east as Athens. In more recent times, Catalans have focused their energies closer to home – in the late 19th century Catalonia became one of Spain's first industrialised regions, known for its textiles.

Montserrat inland from Barcelona, provide a near constant backdrop to the coast – the Costa Brava (Wild Coast) in the north and the Costa Dorada (Golden Coast) farther south. Inland, the mountains continue almost uninterrupted as far as the southern Pyrenees, their flanks furrowed by rushing torrents and lush green valleys. The landscape is often spectacular. At the north end of the Costa Brava, for example, the granite outcrop of the Serra de Roses rises abruptly from the shore, with dizzying overhangs reaching some 3000 feet.

Coming from a largely barren mountain homeland,

the Catalans have always had to live by their wits, and this has meant turning to the sea and commerce. Their days of greatest glory – of which modern Catalans are still acutely aware – started in the 12th century after Catalonia merged with Aragon to the west. The new kingdom of Aragon-Catalonia included large parts of southern France and soon colonised the Balearic Islands. After that, its traders and seamen ventured farther afield in the Mediterranean until, the saying went, 'even the fish bore the colours of Catalonia'. Their influence spread to Sardinia, Sicily (where the

The centre of rural Catalan life, particularly in the north and east, is the masía, *a large, solidly built farmhouse with just two or three windows on the ground floor and the main living quarters on the floor above.*

people of Alghero still speak a form of Catalan), Malta and even Athens. Though never quite on a par with the Italian city states of Genoa and Venice, the Catalans were still among the Mediterranean's greatest trading powers, with consuls in 57 cities.

In 1469, the marriage of Ferdinand of Aragon to Isabella of Castile in central Spain – the future *Reyes Católicos*, 'Catholic Monarchs' – spelt the end of this golden age. From then on the Catalans would find their interests increasingly subordinated to those of the newly emerging kingdom of Spain. At the same time, with the discovery of America by Columbus, the Mediterranean lost much of its economic importance. Even so the Catalans kept a tight grasp on their sense of nationhood, and never lost their industriousness, as well as the characteristic Catalan virtues of common sense, balance and shrewd judgment, which are summed up in the local word *seny*.

In the late 19th century Catalonia became one of Spain's first industrialised regions specialising, above all, in textiles – it was also a stronghold of the various anarchist, communist and socialist parties of the Spanish Left. When the Spanish Republic was declared in 1931, after the abdication of King Alfonso XIII, Catalonia declared itself an autonomous region. Later it was among the chief battlegrounds of the Spanish Civil War (1936-9), with Barcelona one of the last cities to fall to General Franco's Nationalists. Franco did his best to destroy its culture – forbidding, for example, the use of the Catalan language in public – but to little effect. Within months of his death in 1975, Catalan had replaced Castilian (Spanish) on the region's signposts, public notices and the like, and two years later Catalonia regained a measure of autonomy from Madrid, with its own government (*Generalitat*).

But the Catalans are not just a nation of traders. They also have a strong peasant tradition to which they have brought the same enterprising spirit seen in their

The Roman author Pliny had a fondness for the wines of Aragon, and Don Quixote's faithful attendant Sancho Panza spoke yearningly of the wines of Ciudad Real in central Spain, but many modern connoisseurs give the wines of Catalonia pride of place. These include the white wine of Alella, the oaky reds and whites of Penedès and a variety of Champagne-like sparkling wines. Be careful if you try to drink Catalan wines in the local manner from a spouted porrón *– in novice hands the precious liquid is more likely to go down the neck than into the mouth.*

commerce. A Spanish saying has it that the Catalans can make bread from stone, and they certainly make remarkably productive use of their land. In the mountains every green ledge and gully is carefully cultivated. In the north and east, the *tierras de regadío* ('irrigable lands'), they make ingenious use of often unreliable mountain streams and rivers to irrigate the land. In the wetter south and the Llobregat valley are the *tierras de secano*, where vines and almond and olive trees are cultivated without irrigation.

The poet Lorca described the Ramblas of Barcelona as 'the one street in the world which I wish would never end'. The city's most famous thoroughfare, linking the centre with the harbour front, is constantly busy with people. They come to take a leisurely drink in one of the cafés or bars, gather round street performers, buy flowers or caged birds at one of the street stalls, or simply enjoy a paseo (stroll) with friends or family.

The Sardana of Catalonia is one of Spain's most stately regional dances, with roots in the pagan past. There are two basic steps, one short, the other prolonged, which correspond to the rhythm of the music. The musicians setting the pace are called the cobla.

Vegetation and stonework mingle strangely in one of Gaudí's most extravagant creations, the Parc Güell in northern Barcelona. It is an extraordinary confection of tunnelled cloisters, curving lines and gaudy mosaics made from chipped tiles and broken pieces of pottery.

The heart of the city is its most famous thoroughfare, the tree-lined Ramblas which stretches from Plaça de Catalunya in the centre to the shoreline Passeig de Colom (Columbus). During the day, stallholders sell bright arrays of flowers and the caged birds without whose cheerful-sounding trillings no Spanish city would be complete. In the evenings, friends and families meet in the Ramblas for the statutory pre-dinner stroll or *paseo*. Spreading to the east, meanwhile, is the oldest part of the city, the labyrinthine Barri Gotic (Gothic Quarter), dominated by the cathedral, mostly built between 1298 and 1448. To the south-east are the narrow streets of the Barri Xinès (Chinatown) red-light district, with the heights of Montjuïc rising beyond.

From the Palau Nacional broad flights of steps descend to the geometric sweep of the Ensanche area, spreading up towards the slopes of Tibidabo, the 1745-foot hill that backs Barcelona. Here the character of the city changes altogether. Gone are the gypsies, Andalucian workers, prostitutes and cheap *tascas*, *tabernas* and *bodegas* of the Barri Xinès and the quarters of the Old City. In their place, Parisian-style apartment blocks line the two great boulevards of the Gran Via de les Corts Catalanes and Avinguda Diagonal, and the lesser avenues leading off them. Bars (often called 'pubs', though bearing little relation to anything a British visitor would recognise by that name) gleam with glass and chromium plate.

Yet this is still Barcelona. Rising north of the Diagonal are the strange, knobbly spires of the city's greatest landmark, the Templo de la Sagrada Familia (Temple of the Holy Family), started in 1882 on classical lines and taken over a year later by the

In matters of inheritance, the strictest primogeniture rules: the first-born, male or female, inherits the family holding. Indeed, in the country that gave birth to the words *macho* (literally, 'male') and *machismo* ('maleness'), Catalonia stands out, as in so many other areas, for the more or less equal status women have long enjoyed with men.

Europe's most fashionable city

If the *Sardana,* the expressive public dance, is a ritual symbol for the Catalan nation, then Barcelona is the national spirit set forth in stones and mortar: a city of huge vitality, austere and sensual at the same time; rooted in the glories of the past yet frequently in the vanguard of cultural and political movements; pragmatic, commercial and yet with a streak of romance. It is also Spain's largest port, its second-largest city, vaunted in recent years as 'Europe's most fashionable city', and chosen as the site of the 1992 Olympics.

Decorative details drip from Gaudí's Sagrada Familia, the great temple on which he started work in 1883 and which was still far from complete at his death over 40 years later in 1926. Indeed, Gaudí himself believed it would take at least 200 years to finish and concentrated on the east front, so that it could serve as a model for the rest.

*The arum lily – calla –
flourishes throughout Spain's
rainy northern regions, from
Catalonia to Galicia. It is
particularly striking on the
slopes rising from the fjord-
like rías bajas of southern
Galicia, where in spring the
air is thick with the flower's
heady scent.*

*Of all the great religious
festivals, Semana Santa (Holy
Week) is celebrated with most
fervour in Spain. Penitents
parade through the streets of
towns and cities, their faces
covered with veil-like shawls
or the eerie pointed hoods of
the south, while musicians
and drummers beat out
mournful accompaniments. In
the little town of Calanda in
Aragon (birthplace of the
film-maker Buñuel) relays of
drummers keep up the beat
for 24 hours without stopping,
creating a truly apocalyptic
sense of doom.*

32-year-old architectural genius and religious mystic Antoni Gaudí, who turned it into something far from classical. It is still under construction and is likely to remain so for decades, if not centuries, to come. Even so, you can easily make out behind the scaffolding just what an extraordinary building it is, opulent and provocative, adorned in every nook and cranny with sculpted plants, animals and religious inscriptions.

Gaudí was a product of one of the most exuberant eras of Barcelona's recent history, roughly the decades on either side of the turn of the century. It was a period, brewing up for the turmoils of the 1930s, when the city was alive with political, nationalist and cultural activity. The young Picasso, though originally from Málaga, lived here for nine years before moving to Paris, and the works of his 'Blue Period' date from these years – many are now housed in the Picasso Museum in the Old City. Among his friends at the time were the surrealist painters Salvador Dalí and Joan Miró, both Catalans. Meanwhile, architects such as Gaudí were at the forefront of the Art Nouveau movement, whose sinuous lines ornamented with elongated leaves, flowers and birds have left such a strong mark on the city's cafés, theatres and parks.

Catalan ways

Catalan is the language of Barcelona – as it is, in varying degrees, of Valencia beyond Catalonia to the south, the tiny Pyrenean principality of Andorra and Majorca, Minorca and the other Balearic Islands. Not all the inhabitants of Catalonia, however, are Catalan-speakers. Catalonia's prosperity in the 19th century and today is due in large measure to workers who emigrated there from the poorest Spanish regions of the south, notably Murcia and Andalucía. The last great wave arrived in the 1940s – encouraged by Franco who saw it as a way of diluting Catalan culture. And to an extent this ploy worked. The immigrants, who form the bulk of the unskilled workforce, do not share the nationalist sentiments of the fiercely Catalan skilled workers and upper social strata.

On the other hand, they have had little impact on the countryside, where people's ways are still impregnated with the region's traditional culture. Rising in the heart of this is yet another totem of the Catalan nation, the small, jagged range of Montserrat ('serrated mountain'), whose steep ravines and pink-tinged rocky outcrops were once a favoured retreat for hermits; they now offer tourists superb views on fine days as far as the Pyrenees to the north and Aragon to the west.

But, above all, the range is home to the mysterious black Virgin of Montserrat, the *Moreneta*. Every year some 50,000 pilgrims make their way up the mountains to the 19th-century basilica, in order to venerate a small wooden statue kept in a glass case above the high altar. The story goes that it was sculpted by St Luke and brought to Barcelona by St Peter. Later, it was hidden at Montserrat to keep it safe from the Muslim Moors who invaded Spain in the 8th century, and then miraculously rediscovered by shepherds in 880. Given such supposed precedents, it is not surprising that the statue is believed to have extraordinary powers.

Lonely Aragon

Heading west from Catalonia into Aragon, the landscape changes. The mountain ranges retreat north towards the central spine of the Pyrenees, leaving wide,

Mountain slopes rise vertiginously from the Cantabrian coast in the region of Asturias, with villages such as Luarca clinging to their sides. This remote, once impenetrable region was the launching place of the Reconquista, *after the Gothic chieftain Pelayo had defeated a small force of Moorish troops at Covadonga in AD 718.*

open plains such as the *hoya* (valley) of Huesca, the northernmost of the Aragonese provinces. It is a bleakly impressive, largely empty countryside, constructed on a gigantic scale, where expanses of plain or low, rolling hills spread on and on as far as the eye can see, and a kind of dun brown prevails. Towns and villages are rare, and many of the dwellings in them deserted, their former occupants having left for cities such as Barcelona to seek a better living. Old noble palaces – relics of Aragon-Catalonia's days of glory – are elaborately decorated with coats of arms, sculpted figures and wrought-iron balconies, but the *hidalgos* (minor noblemen) who once lived in the them have long since departed.

In northern Huesca the district around Jaca, lying in the rain shadow of the Pyrenees, is renowned for its dryness. Far to the south, the province of Teruel rises to the arid steppes of Spain's central plateau and Castile. Here lie some of the loneliest parts of Aragon. It is splendid hiking country, where you can walk around places such as Las Bardenas and Los Monegros for a whole day without meeting a soul or hearing a human voice. In winter this area is bitterly cold with icy, dry winds whipping in from the north. The regions between these two extremes are more smiling, irrigated by rivers such as the Ebro (Spain's mightiest river, rising in the Cantabrian Mountains of the north and reaching the Mediterranean south of Tarragona) and producing rich crops of wine grapes, olives, cereals and sugar cane.

As befits such a landscape, the Aragonese (nicknamed *baturros*, literally 'people who are rough or uncouth') are a serious-minded race, often rather brusque in their manner. They are no compromisers,

unlike their neighbours the Catalans who take the world as they find it and seek to gain what profit they can. Instead, the Aragonese will stubbornly defend any point of view they hold. They, too, have produced some remarkable figures: the great painter Francisco de Goya; the film-maker Luis Buñuel; and the Saura brothers, Carlos (a film-maker) and Antonio (a painter).

Aragon's capital, also containing half the region's population of 1.2 million people, is Saragossa (Zaragoza). One of its two cathedrals houses Spain's most venerated Virgin, the *Virgen del Pilar* (of the Pillar), after whom so many Spanish women are named. The pillar in question is ensconced in a niche in the *Catedral Nuestra Señora del Pilar*'s huge Lady Chapel, and the story goes that the Virgin Mary appeared to St James the Apostle on top of it. She is celebrated with great pomp in the *Fiesta del Pilar* every October, when the city gives itself up to an orgy of processions, dancing the Aragonese *jota* and bullfights.

Bull runs in Navarre

In the north-west, Aragon merges into the old kingdom of Navarre (Navarra), whose territories like those of Aragon once extended beyond the Pyrenees into southern France. Indeed, for many centuries until 1512, when Spanish Navarre was annexed by Castile, the kingdom was ruled by a succession of French dynasties, among whose descendants was Henry IV 'of Navarre', the first Bourbon king of France. The people of Navarre are deeply aware of their ancient heritage and traditions, and are among the most conservative in Spain.

Crowds milling in the streets of Pamplona before the bull running, or encierro; *many wear the traditional white shirts and red berets. The* encierro *is an extraordinary display, mingling courage with bravado, the sublime with the absurd. At eight each morning, during the nine days of the* Sangermines, *the bulls are let loose on a circuit of streets just over a mile long. Spectators gather behind wooden palings or on balconies, while runners congregate in the streets ready for the onslaught of the bulls.*

The fishing port of Pasajes, sheltering at the feet of high cliffs on the Cantabrian coast, has one of the best natural harbours of the Basque Country. About 200 vessels are based here, of which some 40 regularly cross the Atlantic as far as the cod-rich banks of Newfoundland. With San Sebastián and Fuenterrabía, it is one of the three most important fishing bases along this stretch of coast – about a million tons of fish pass through it each year.

The beret and red neckscarf are still everyday wear for older Navarrese men. They come from a hardy, conservative race, claimed by some to be descended from warriors who fought for the ancient Carthiginians against the Romans. Later, they put up stout resistance against the Visigoths who arrived in Spain in the declining years of the Roman Empire, and later again, in the 9th century, set up their own kingdom which included parts of southern France.

Navarre falls into two fairly distinct halves, the mountainous north spreading up into the Pyrenees, the south extending in fertile plains as far as the Ebro. Wheat and cereal crops cover most of the south, which is one of Spain's granaries, while vines and olives grow up the slopes of its hillier parts – it is very like the wine region of La Rioja beyond the Ebro. But Navarre is probably most famous for its capital Pamplona (or Iruña) and Pamplona's great *Fiesta de San Fermín* which is held between July 6 and 14 each year. Visitors converge on the city from the four corners of Spain as well as abroad to take part in, or at least watch, the extraordinary spectacle of the *encierro,* the running of the bulls. The American novelist Ernest Hemingway was one person who never missed a chance to take part, often spending the nights sleeping rough in the streets and celebrating the event in his novel *Fiesta (The Sun Also Rises).*

Of all Spain's many great *fiestas,* the *Sanfermines* and the *encierro* in particular are certainly among the most startling. At about eight o'clock each morning the six bulls that will later that day face the *toreros* in the *plaza de toros* (bullring) are let loose into a circuit of streets that have been carefully palisaded off from the rest of the city. Dense crowds of people await them here – traditionally men only, though in recent years some women have also joined in the fun. They run alongside the bulls, taunting and baiting them, and then scatter in mad confusion, scrambling for the relative safety of the palisades when the enraged beasts charge. There is at least one serious accident each year, and often more – one year more than 70 people were injured; another year, a single bull gored three people to death.

Why do it? The answer seems to be that the challenge of the *encierro* represents much that the traditional Spanish *macho* most admires – there is the courage required, the strange (if for many non-Spanish people disturbing) beauty of the occasion, the sense that life and death are to be held lightly so long as you confront them with honour and style. Elsewhere in Spain it is the *torero* who lives out these fantasies in the bullring; in Pamplona the man in the street can show that he too is as brave as, if not braver than, the *torero*. In fact, all these things are still so deeply ingrained in the Spanish character that if you asked a runner why he and his friends were doing it, he would probably reply with disarming simplicity: *Porque somos españoles* (Because we're Spanish).

For all the industrial might of Bilbao and Vitoria, the Basque Country remains a largely agricultural region. In the north, fruit orchards and livestock clothe the green mountain sides. Here, in the flatter south, wheat fields cover large acres, while flocks of sheep graze stretches of pasture shaded by occasional copses of pines.

The region of the Basques

Spanish regionalism is more marked than that of almost any other western European nation, and nowhere is it more noticeable than at either end of the mountain barrier of the Pyrenees. Here, two distinctive races – the Catalans and the Basques – enjoy ties with kinsmen north of the French border that are in many ways as strong as their ties with the rest of Spain. This is especially true of the Basques at the Atlantic end, bound into an exceptionally close-knit group with a language that bears no generally accepted relation to any other known tongue and ancestral roots that remain a mystery.

The Basques' homeland (Euskadi), which within Spain includes northern Navarre as well as the three provinces of Guipúzcoa, Vizcaya and Alava, is one of great beauty. In the east, forests, the home of a few rare bears and wolves, descend from the summits of the Navarrese Pyrenees, giving way on the lower slopes to a pastoral landscape of apple orchards and pastureland grazed by sheep and cattle. This area has one of the most famous gateways into Spain, the pass of Roncesvalles. In AD 778, a Basque army ambushed the rearguard of the Emperor Charlemagne's army at Roncesvalles as it returned to France after a raid on Spain. The event has been celebrated, and much elaborated, from both sides: in the 12th-century French epic poem *The Song of Roland* (which turns the Basques into Moors and gives the heroic role to Charlemagne's nephew Roland) and in the Spanish *Poem of Bernardo del Carpio*, named after the Basques' leader.

The three provinces of the west offer rather different scenery. Here, on Spain's northern coast, the landscape is broken with abruptly rising hills and mountains which plunge dramatically along their northern edge into the Bay of Biscay. Rain clouds roll in regularly from the sea, shrouding the land in a fine, tenacious drizzle, a kind of Scotch mist known here as *chirimiri*, that endows the landscape with a gloriously brilliant green.

The Basque Country, along with Catalonia, was one of Spain's first industrialised regions. But the Basques themselves are an essentially rural people rooted in the traditions of their small, isolated communities. They are proud, independent, wilful, often hot-tempered and very direct. Unlike other Spanish people they tend to be taciturn, but like the rest of Spain their region abounds in local *fiestas* and traditional songs and dances. They are also lovers of good food, especially seafood, to which they dedicate a near-religious devotion – a Spanish proverb has it that the chief concern of the Catalan is to have a fine home, of the Castilian to be well dressed, and of the Basque to eat well. They also have a strongly competitive streak. Local fairs often centre on contests between *aizkolari*, woodcutters who vie with each other to split huge tree trunks, and *harrijasotzaile*, muscle-bound champions heaving huge boulders. Another Basque sport, now popular throughout Spain and the Spanish-speaking world, is *jai-alai*, or *pelota*, played rather like squash in a walled court usually with a scoop-shaped wicker racket or

chistera, though each region has its own variations.

The traditional centre of Basque rural life is the *caserío*, the family farm typically covering only 15 acres or so, with a few arable fields, a small apple orchard, a vegetable plot and some rough pastureland. This imposes quite different patterns of life from those of the more gregarious southern parts of Spain where the large estate or *latifundio* dominates and peasant communities are centred on the village. Here in the Basque Country, each family lives isolated on its *caserío*, having little contact with neighbouring farms scattered over the hill and mountainsides. Work is hard, involving every member of the family – parents, children, grandparents, unmarried aunts and uncles. The rewards are relatively meagre, but the damaging effects of the endless subdivision of smallholdings among different children are avoided by strict conventions of inheritance. Traditionally, the father chooses one of his sons (not necessarily the eldest) to inherit all.

Racial origins

Theories abound as to the origins of the Basques. Some Russian ethnologists have maintained that there are distinct similarities, both linguistic and physical, between the Basques and certain remote tribes of Iran and northern Mesopotamia. Others, notably the great Spanish scholar Ramón Menéndez Pidal, have put forward a more elaborate theory: that the Basques are the direct descendants of Cro-Magnon races who inhabited Europe in the late Stone Age before being swamped by Indo-European tribes from the Near East. Whatever the truth of the various theories, the Basques are an extremely ancient race who have survived as a more or less unified group in their mountainous homeland. Amidst the mounting tide of Latin-based tongues, they have kept alive their own beautiful, though extraordinarily complex language, Euskera.

In fact, they have long been ruthless in preserving their identity. In the late 19th century, factors such as improved communications and, paradoxically, the success of Basque industry (bringing with it immigrants from elsewhere in Spain) threatened to swamp Basque integrity. Nationalists, taking their cue from the romantic movement throughout Europe, set about reviving ancient traditions and inventing a few new ones. They even went to the extent of creating a new national hero, Aïtor, and an epic poem, the *Altobiscar*, another retelling of the story of Roncesvalles from the Basque point of view. They also pieced together a new name for their land, Euskadi.

A long face and dark hair are the marks of the typical Basque. The Basques also tend to be taller than other Spanish people, and the men are famed for their strength – which they love to demonstrate at local fairs in woodcutting and weightlifting contests.

The rare black grouse, found in a few wooded areas of the mountains of Ancares between León and Galicia, is a much sought-after prize for hunters. Its rasping cry can sometimes be heard echoing through the mountains – sending local enthusiasts scrambling in its pursuit.

In the 20th century Basque nationalism became an overtly political movement seeking autonomy for Euskadi. During the Civil War, the Basques of Guipúzcoa, Vizcaya and Alava, unlike their kinsmen in Navarre, sided with the Republicans – and the town of Guernica in particular paid a heavy price for so doing. On April 26, 1937, aircraft of Franco's Nazi German allies bombed it on market day, killing more than 2000 people, an episode which caused widespread revulsion throughout the world. Picasso's painting *Guernica* became a symbol of the horrors of war. Franco later sought to crush Basque culture, but as in Catalonia succeeded only in stiffening it. The terrorist group ETA (*Euskadi ta Azkatasuna* – Freedom for Euskadi) waged constant war against Madrid.

The coming of democracy has brought huge improvements for the Basques. They now have their own parliament and police force, and their language – which only a few years ago seemed in irreversible decline – is thriving once more, taught in half the region's primary schools. Yet still there are the die-hard nationalists who want more. ETA, though to some extent brought under control, continues its bombings and demands for complete independence.

Cantabria – heartland of the Reconquista

West of the Basque Country, 'green' Spain spreads on along the Cantabrian Coast, with the Cantabrian Mountains – after Switzerland, Spain is Europe's most

A Galician peasant takes home a cartload of seaweed for use as fertiliser. Ox carts such as this are common in Galicia, where smallholdings, or minifundios, *are often very small indeed and the rewards for working them meagre. Like their kinsmen the Portuguese, the Galicians often carry heavy loads on their heads – indeed, in the 18th century, according to one British traveller, the women used to 'carry the men across the rivers on their heads in a basket'.*

Spanish men are famous for their machismo *– but in fact theirs is a profoundly matriarchal society. In the north, it is the woman (left) who not only runs the household but also does the buying and selling and looks after the family finances. In many regions, the peasant woman also has the chief say in what crops are grown and livestock raised.*

The pallozas *of the remote Ancares region between León and Galicia are ancient, windowless dwellings still used as homes by some of the region's older inhabitants. Until recently, Ancares was more or less cut off from the rest of Spain by its inaccessible terrain and poor roads. This left it a paradise for wild animals such as boars and deer, which are still abundant there.*

mountainous country – rising inland to peaks well over 6500 feet high and in the Picos de Europa reaching 8826 feet. The two provinces centred on the cities of Santander and Oviedo correspond roughly to the historic regions of Asturias and the Montaña of Castile, wild country left largely untouched by both the Romans and Moors. As a result it formed a perfect launching place for the long, painful process of the *Reconquista*, by which the Spanish regained control of their peninsula from the Moors. During the *Reconquista*, which started in the 8th century and was completed only in the 15th, these regions also provided many of the first settlers of the newly reconquered lands of the peninsula's high central plateau, the Meseta.

The coastal scenery here is dramatic, with ancient villages and towns sheltering between high cliffs and the sea – places such as Castro-Urdiales, founded in Roman times and priding itself on being the oldest of all the towns along the Cantabrian Coast. But the real gem is Santillana del Mar, a glorious sanctuary of narrow streets, noble palaces and churches. Santillana was once an important stopping-off point on the Pilgrims' Way to Santiago. Its Colegiata church also housed the remains of St Juliana, a martyr of the early church, making it a place of pilgrimage in its own right. In the late Middle

The baroque pinnacles of Santiago cathedral's west front rise gloriously above the city. Although the interior is medieval, the outside was almost completely reworked in the 17th and 18th centuries. The west front is one of the finest examples of the Churrigueresque style, named after the architect and sculptor José Churriguera and notable for its sumptuous elaboration of ornament and detail.

Ages it was the seat of the powerful Marquises of Santillana, key figures in the *Reconquista*, and many of Spain's most aristocratic families claim descent from the first inhabitants of its palaces.

Inland and to the west, meanwhile, rise the Picos de Europa, a dramatic region of towering limestone summits, separated by plunging gorges, and fine walking country. This, too, is rich in memories of the *Reconquista*. It was here that the rebel Spanish leader Pelayo sought refuge with a handful of followers after the Moors first swept into Spain in AD 711. And it was at Covadonga in the west of the Picos that Pelayo scored a small, but symbolically important, victory over the invaders in 718 – regarded as the starting point of the *Reconquista*. He went on to establish the kingdom of Asturias, the first independent kingdom of post-Moorish Spain and the cradle of the country's monarchy, which still gives the king's eldest son the title of Príncipe de las Asturias.

St James and Galicia

Galicia – not to be confused with the region of the same name in central Europe – is the north-western corner of Spain, wedged between the Bay of Biscay to the north,

the Atlantic to the west and Portugal to the south. It is famous above all for the great pilgrim city of Santiago de Compostela (St James of Compostela). It is also one of Spain's most intriguing regions, quite different from the rest of the peninsula. Physically, it is a damp, lushly green region, fringed by the sea, with wide stretches of open moor and rough pastureland in an interior that is more reminiscent of Brittany, Cornwall, Wales or Ireland than the other Spanish *costas*. The geographical similarity is all the more striking because the Galicians, or Gallegos, are in fact Celts, like the Bretons, Cornish, Welsh and Irish – and, for that matter, the Galicians of Poland and the Galatians of ancient Asia Minor.

As in Cornwall and Brittany, the call of the sea and seafaring is strong in Galicia, as is the sense of mystery and romance usually associated with the mariner's life. The enigmatic world of the Druids does not seem so far away in a land where orthodox Christianity has yet to eliminate beliefs and customs dating from pagan times. In Galicia, priests still bless springs and animals; peasants still regard certain oak groves as holy places; and some seamen still testify to an almost religious sense of awe in the face of the great ocean stretching out from their region's western shore – just as the Roman legionaries did when they first reached Cape Finisterre, considered the end of the world, *finis terrae*.

But Galicia's appeal is not just that of romance. Any Spanish person will assure you that it is one of their

Feiras (markets) see Galician women at their liveliest. Everything can be bought there from vegetables, fruit, meat and seafood to clothes and household goods. But perhaps the most enjoyable aspect – for outsiders at least – is the gallery of local characters they offer.

Lace is the most famous product of the Galician town of Camariñas. The townspeople learnt their skills from Flemish lacemakers in the 17th century, when local merchants carried on an important trade with the Low Countries, and their style has not changed since then.

In the Middle Ages, the cockleshell was the emblem of the pilgrim who had made the journey to Santiago. According to one legend, the custom arose after a local noble had to swim across a ría *to escape his Moorish enemies; when he emerged on the other side, he was covered all over with cockleshells.*

country's most beautiful regions, and is then likely to expound on its sublime views of sea, mountains and meandering rivers, its misty tints of green and blue, and its great expanses of pine forest. He or she is equally likely to continue: 'I'd really like to get to know it.' For the truth is that Galicia is nowadays one of Spain's least-known regions. Not that this was always so. In the Middle Ages, Santiago was, with Jerusalem, one of the two most important centres of pilgrimage in Christian Europe, believed to house the remains of the Apostle St James the Great. Among the many thousands of pilgrims who followed the long, often perilous, *Camino de Santiago* (Way of St James) on foot, horseback or in primitive carriages were future saints (such as Francis of Assisi and Thomas Becket), great rulers (such as Charlemagne), and, in fiction, Chaucer's Wife of Bath.

The world has changed, of course, since then, but one place the medieval pilgrims might just recognise is the mountain district of Ancares in the east, on Galicia's borders with Asturias and the Castilian province of León. Until very recent decades, the absence of any decent roads kept Ancares preserved in a kind of time lock where, quite literally, the patterns of life had scarcely changed since the Middle Ages (the only parallel in Spain is the equally remote district of Las Hurdes, near the Portuguese border west of Madrid, whose tragic under-development was chronicled in the 1930s by Luis Buñuel). Some roads have now been built to Ancares – but too late. Its villages are fast dying, if not dead already. Most of the young people have left for Barcelona or the Americas. Only the old remain, some still living in extraordinary, primitive dwellings known as *pallozas*.

The *palloza* is a circular building, typically 30 feet or more in diameter with walls that can be up to 10 feet high, and topped by a conical, steeply sloping, thatched roof. It serves for everything – kitchen, bedroom, barn and storehouse. Here, the family share quarters in winter with their three or four cows, calves, pigs

(slaughtered at the start of winter to provide meat for the rest of the year), hay to feed the animals, potato stocks and farming implements.

Farther west, beyond the bleak *sierras* (mountain ranges) of the eastern borderlands, you reach the lush Galicia of the Spanish imagination, where fjord-like *rías* spread their fingers far inland and long, golden strands of beach may tempt the unwary visitor to brave their icy, Atlantic waters. It is certainly glorious country to explore – and not just the cities, mostly congregated on the coastal strip. Some 75 per cent of the Galician population still lives in rural communities, and it is now a relatively easy matter to leave the main roads, plunge down minor ones and delve around among tiny market towns and villages where life, though not as harsh as that of Ancares, preserves many ancient ways.

But of course the cities are also there, and they too reflect the life of Galicia: Lugo in the centre, founded by the Romans; Vigo, Spain's most important fishing port, in the south; La Coruña (or Corunna in English); and, above all, Santiago. In fact, Compostela, situated as it is at the end of Europe, was a centre of pilgrimage before Christianity arrived in Galicia; the legend of St James simply fitted neatly around the existing pagan beliefs. According to the legend, St James came to Spain after Christ's death to convert its people to the new faith, and spent seven years there before returning to Jerusalem where he was martyred by Herod (his martyrdom, at least, is a historical truth). Then, the story continues, his followers brought his body back to Spain and buried it near the spot in Galicia where he had first landed on the peninsula.

The grave was then forgotten for several centuries until a star is said to have led some shepherds to it in 813. And at that point the legend of *Santiago Matamoros* (Killer of the Moors) was born. The Spanish of the *Reconquista* had a champion worthy to take on the Prophet Muhammad, whose memory inspired the Muslim Moors to such extraordinary feats. In 844,

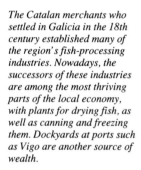

The Catalan merchants who settled in Galicia in the 18th century established many of the region's fish-processing industries. Nowadays, the successors of these industries are among the most thriving parts of the local economy, with plants for drying fish, as well as canning and freezing them. Dockyards at ports such as Vigo are another source of wealth.

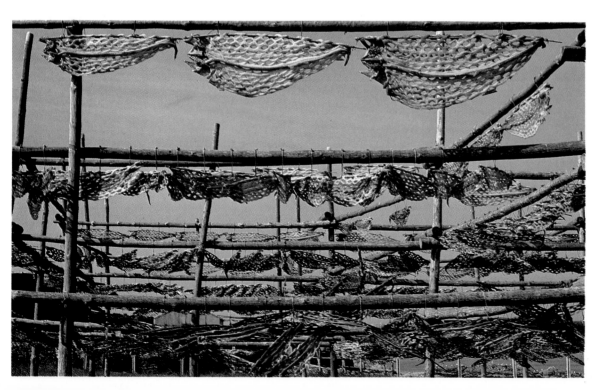

during the battle of Clavijo in northern Castile, a mysterious knight carrying a white standard with a red cross on it was reported to come into the fray on the side of King Ramiro I of Asturias. Almost single-handedly he beat back the 'infidel' Moors, and after the battle it was generally agreed that the knight had been none other than St James. After that, many similar miraculous events were reported. A chapel, then a church and, finally, today's glorious cathedral were built around the grave said to contain his remains.

Land of farewell

Throughout the centuries, Galicia has been a land of departures. In the days of empire that followed the *Reconquista,* the Galicians provided their contingents for the peopling of the New World. And the pattern of emigration has continued. It is estimated that more than 400,000 people left the region in the 18th century, and a million during the 19th century. Between 1900 and 1965, Galicia lost 1.5 million inhabitants. Most went to the Americas, and Galicians speak with a slightly melancholy pride of the largest Galician city in the world: Buenos Aires, with more than a million Galician inhabitants. More recently emigration has tended to flow towards the rest of Europe. The result has been a 1 per cent fall in the region's population, during a period in which that of Spain as a whole has grown by 21 per

cent. The reasons for the exodus are clear enough. They can be seen in the region's primitive agricultural methods, its antique ploughs and in the arduous hand labour (generally carried out by women) of tiny smallholdings (*minifundios*).

This chronic state of under-development helps to explain the Galicians' reputation as reserved, rather mistrustful people, who dislike committing themselves to anything. According to other Spanish people, a Galician always answers a question with another question – when you meet one on a staircase you are never sure whether he is coming up or going down. In fact, most Galicians are good-natured, with a sharp sense of humour. Since the men are so often at sea or abroad, the women are used to ordering family affairs. And it is they who transmit the region's traditions from generation to generation. The austerity characteristic of the Castilians has no place among their kinsmen in Galicia. Not for them the barefoot asceticism of Castile's religious festivals – instead, their *fiestas* and *romerías* (open-air festivals or pilgrimages) are marked by a sensuous delight in the whole occasion which often ends at dawn in pagan fashion.

To come properly to grips with the Galicians, it helps to know their language, spoken by 80 per cent of the population. Gallego is an attractive tongue, softer and more melodious than Castilian, like Portuguese. Indeed, until the 15th century, Gallego and Portuguese were the same language. But the drifting apart of Galicia and

Corunna (La Coruña), a substantial port before Roman times, boasts the Tower of Hercules, the only Roman lighthouse in the world that is still in use. The port also has a place in British history. The Spanish Armada called at Corunna during its disastrous voyage to England in 1588. And in 1809, during the Peninsular War, it was the scene of Sir John Moore's famous rearguard action against the French troops of Marshal Soult. This allowed the bulk of the British army to embark safely on ships bound for England.

Portugal combined with centralising pressure from Madrid have separated the two tongues. In this century Gallego was banned in public under Franco – though he himself was Galician. Yet, despite the divergences between their two languages, Galicians and Portuguese can still understand one another.

Although the return of democracy has brought something of a renaissance of Gallego, Galicia's relative poverty means that its language – unlike Basque or Catalan – is still often seen as one of the underdog, of peasants, labourers and seamen. This is a curious reversal of what used to be. In the Spanish kingdoms of the early Middle Ages, it was Gallego that was the language of culture and Castilian that of everyday reality. In the 13th century, Alfonso X ('the Wise'), born at Toledo far to the south in central Castile, used Castilian for promulgating his laws and decrees, but Gallego for his poetry. Only after the Catholic Monarchs had brought the whole of Spain under their joint rule did Gallego's importance decline.

The death fixation

The Galicians have a strange fascination with death, as many of their legends attest. One of these is the legend of the *Santa Compaña*, a procession of souls from Purgatory who come to mingle with the spirits of the living and those yet to be born, trooping at midnight of any day of the week except Sunday along little-frequented local roads (or *corredoiras*). If you encounter them you must never accept a candle offered by one of these lost souls – or you too will be swept into their company. Keep your fists firmly clenched and mutter a few Ave Marias until you reach the safety of your home. Less dangerous for the casual passer-by are the processions of the living-dead at Puebla del Caramiñal and Santa Marta. The former takes place in mid-September. In a ritual dating from the 15th century, people who believe they have been saved from death by divine intervention follow an empty coffin through the streets to the local cemetery. At Santa Marta, the ceremony (which takes place on July 29) is still more macabre. Those who have been saved by a miracle lie in open coffins and are borne to the cemetery on the shoulders of their weeping families.

According to one modern Spanish scholar, Novoa Santos, this curious Galician death-wish is a manifestation of the people's poetic nature: 'The instinctive will to die reveals itself only among people with a subtle poetic instinct, mixed with the feeling of *saudade*.' *Saudade*, which the Galicians share with the Portuguese, is a characteristic local affliction for which there is no satisfactory English word. Roughly, it is homesickness, but in Galicia homesickness has two grades – there is *morriña*, a relatively mild complaint, and *saudade* which is altogether more serious. *Morriña* can be cured by going home, but *saudade* can become a yearning for death, a desire to return to the land in the most ultimate sense.

With their menfolk at sea or working in one of Spain's industrial cities or abroad, Galician women have to do most of the work on their tiny minifundios. Of course, some families are lucky. They strike it rich in their jobs or businesses abroad (traditionally America) and return to build the modern homes that dot Galician villages. These may be the envy of their owners' neighbours, but they somewhat mar the landscape for the tourist.

Dry Lands Under the Mediterranean Sun

Valencia on the Levante coast of eastern Spain – and the country's third largest city – is the setting for another great *fiesta*: the *Fallas* of San José (St Joseph), which takes place between March 17 and 19. The festival began in the 15th century as a celebration by local carpenters of the coming of spring and longer days, which would enable them to work without the help of artificial light. On the feast day of their patron saint Joseph they would make a heap of the wooden batons, or *estais*, which they used to hang oil lamps over their work benches, and set fire to them. These bonfires were known as *fallas*, from the Latin *facula*, or 'torch'.

Over the centuries the *fallas* became a celebration for all Valencians not just the carpenters, and effigies of unpopular local figures were added to the bonfires – rather as guys are burnt on Bonfire Night in England. Gradually these developed into the hugely elaborate pasteboard floats that you now see, with grotesque, garishly painted caricatures not just of locals but also of national and international figures.

These are the work of long, anxious nights and weekends throughout the year. Each quarter of the city has its own float, and rivalry is intense. Committees are formed, plans made and no expense is spared, with budgets often running into the equivalent of thousands of pounds. For a quarter to win the prize for best *falla* is an honour beyond price.

During the three days of the festival Valencia gives itself over to an orgy of dancing, singing, feasting and bullfighting – naturally no work is even contemplated. No one sleeps for three days and the uproar is incessant, with *tracas* – cords strung across the streets and hung with small explosive cartridges – constantly going off in deafening bursts of gunpowder. Then come the crowning moments of the last night. The prizes have been awarded, and at ten o'clock the smaller floats are set alight. Finally, at midnight the most important *fallas* go up in flames. People at last go bleary-eyed to bed, and teams of workmen start clearing up. By the morning of March 20 the streets are impeccable. Nothing remains of the bonfires or the litter of the revels. Everything has to be re-created for the following year.

The Levante coast has been the meeting point of more cultural cross-currents than any other part of the country. Among its first settlers were the original Iberians, tribesmen related to the modern Berbers who crossed from North Africa in prehistoric times. Later came the galleys of Phoenician, Greek and Carthaginian traders, all of whom established colonies on its low shoreline. They were succeeded by the Romans and

Oranges are the principal crop of the Costa del Azahar (literally, 'Coast of the Orange Blossom'), which stretches north from Valencia to Castellón. The fertile soils and warm, sunny climate of the Levante region are especially suitable for the orange tree.

White doves scatter in one of Valencia's main squares. The awning above indicates that the city is preparing for one of its many fiestas. *These include the* Fallas *in mid-March; the* Fiestas de Mayo *(May), celebrating the* Virgen de los Desamparados *(of the Helpless), in which floral displays are a special feature; the processions of* Corpus Christi; *and two* Ferias *(Fairs), one in summer, the other in autumn.*

later the Visigoths striking south from modern France, and the Moors moving north from Africa. The Moors established one of their richest kingdoms at Valencia – a tempting prize briefly captured and ruled in the late 11th century by the Christian hero El Cid. Today, resorts such as Benidorm, which only 40 years ago were pretty fishing villages, are concrete jungles catering for yearly invasions of sun-seeking Britons, Germans and Scandinavians.

The attractions of the land are obvious. Narrow coastal plains, backed dramatically by mountains, include some of the most fertile soil in Europe. Citrus groves cover the *huerta* (irrigated land) around Valencia, creating a densely populated landscape of sun-red soil and rich shades of green, best captured by the turn-of-the-century artist Joaquín Sorolla. Farther south, rice paddies lend a Far Eastern touch as they spread out around La Albufera – providing the basic ingredient of the Valencian speciality, *paella*. To the south again, beyond the limits of Valencia province, the *sierras* draw closer to the shore and the land becomes more barren. The silvery sheen of olive groves replaces the dark green of orange trees. In places the scenery recalls the coastline of North Africa with dry gullies breaking through the scrub of rocky, sun-burnt slopes. To complete the effect, palm groves flourish in oasis-like patches of fertility around Cox, Callosa, Orihuela and Elche.

Unlike neighbouring Catalonia, the Valencian region was largely bypassed by the industrial revolution of the late 19th and 20th centuries. As a result it still lives mostly from the wealth of the *huerta*. Water is all-important in this dry, though fertile land, and every

Thursday a ritual dating from the days of the Moors takes place outside the Apostles' Door of the cathedral: it is the meeting of the *Tribunal de las Aguas* (Water Tribunal). This settles disputes over rights to the eight irrigation canals, originally devised by Moorish engineers, which distribute the waters of the Turia river across the *huerta*. The judges are themselves respected peasants from the *huerta,* and by tradition their word is final. The disputants make their cases, and the judges give their judgment. Nothing is written down – no appeal is possible.

The rock of Gibraltar raises its jagged profile against a luminous southern sky. The British captured it in 1704 during the War of the Spanish Succession, and have hung on to it ever since, despite regular protests from the Spanish, because of its strategic importance. In recent years, however, Spain's entry into the European Community and NATO seems to hold out the hope of some resolution of the problem. The rock takes its name – originally Gebel Tarik, or Mountain of Tariq – from Tariq ibn Aeyad, who led the first Moorish force to land in Spain in AD 711.

Whitewashed houses and old women dressed in black sum up the foreigner's picture of Andalucía. Climate, as well as Moorish and other influences, has created the unique Spanish timetable. People prefer to live in the relative coolness of shady streets, and gear their life to avoid the hottest parts of the day – hence, the long afternoon siestas and the late-night hours.

The Andalucian soul

A pass in the Sierra Enmedio in the southern Levante leads into one of the most extraordinary landscapes in Europe, an example of what geologists know graphically as 'badlands'. On all sides, mountains of an eerie, lunar whiteness spread out, covering much of the eastern Andalucian province of Almería in a complex jigsaw of notched ridges and strangely twisting peaks. These *sierras* – formed by deposits of marl clay which have survived the erosion of the ages because there has

never been enough rain to wash them away – are the most arid, and impenetrable, in the whole of Spain. They are also among the most striking, with patterns of unexpected colour traced across the whiteness of the marl where veins of rare minerals emerge onto the surface. In places the scenery is reminiscent of the American Far West, and indeed the Italian director Sergio Leone chose the region to film many of his 'spaghetti' westerns – the derelict sets are now part of Almería's tourist trail.

To the west, Andalucía – the Biblical Tarshish,

Stretching between the Atlantic and the Mediterranean, Andalucía is Spain's richest farming region, yielding a fifth of the national production of cereals, olives and wine. It is blessed with a warm climate, and soil that is fertile when irrigated. Here, in the Sierra Nevada, livestock and forestry (especially pines) are the principal forms of agriculture.

The vast flood plain of the Guadalquivir, near Seville, produces rich crops of cotton, sugar beet, oranges and, in swampy areas, rice. And yet it also has one of the highest levels of agricultural unemployment – land owner-ship is concentrated into the hands of a few families and there is a high degree of mechanisation. Andalucía as a whole, with one sixth of the Spanish population, accounts for a quarter of national unemployment. The average income in the region is half that of the Basque Country.

Roman Baetica and Arabic al Andalus – extends across southern Spain as far as the Gulf of Cadiz on the Atlantic coast. It is by far the largest Spanish region, covering 33,825 square miles (larger than Scotland) with some 7 million inhabitants. It is also the most diverse region in a country notable for its diversity, encompassing the barren lands of central Almería; the high, snow-capped mass of the Sierra Nevada (with mainland Spain's highest peak, the Cerro de Mulhacén – 11,600 feet); the sadly spoiled shoreline of the Costa del Sol around Málaga; the hot, vine-covered slopes around Cádiz and Jerez de la Frontera (home of sherry); and the rich agricultural plains of the Guadalquivir valley and the Campiña of Córdoba.

Many historical currents have come together to form the Andalucian character – above all, eight centuries of Muslim rule. These started in AD 711 when Tariq, Governor of Tangier, crossed the Strait of Gibraltar with 7000 Berber warriors and defeated the Visigothic King Roderic. The Moors have left a deep mark on the region, though a substantial Jewish population also had its influence. The great merit of the new conquerors was their liberal attitude to the cultures of their subject peoples. And under them, Andalucía blossomed not only in commerce and agriculture, but also in the arts and sciences, drawing on the traditions of Muslims, Jews and Christians alike. Their capitals became seats of learning, through which some of the scholarship of the classical world of Greece and Rome, as well as of the outstanding scientists and philosophers of the Muslim world (then considerably more advanced than Christendom), reached medieval Europe.

Though so long departed, their continuing influence can still be felt – in, for example, a certain oriental detachment in the face of life. This has left the people of Andalucía with a marked aloofness from what they regard as trivialities ... such as work, in some cases. For them, the *gana,* the impulsive desire to do the thing that catches their fancy, is all-important. This is a characteristic, indeed, of many Spanish people, an expression of their fiery national pride, but nowhere more than in Andalucía. *Hago lo que me da la gana* – 'I do what I feel like doing' – is a typically Andalucian way of explaining some arbitrary decision. It has not, however, prevented the region from producing men of genius, from the painters Velázquez and Murillo to the poets Luís de Góngora (born in Córdoba in 1561) and Federico García Lorca (shot by the Nationalists at Granada in 1936).

Cities of light

Granada, one of Andalucía's trio of great cities, spreads over three hills on the north-western flank of the Sierra Nevada. It introduces another element to the Andalucian equation – the gypsies, whose troglodite homes pit the hillside of Sacromonte on the north-eastern edge of the city. Spain has one of the largest populations of gypsies of any Western country, and nowhere is their colourful

presence more noticeable than in the south where they add yet another non-European influence – which is felt, above all, in the alien, though utterly hypnotic, rhythms of flamenco.

But, of course, Granada is most famous for its Moorish past. It has the glorious 14th-century Moorish palace of the Alhambra, a labyrinth of richly mosaiced halls and courtyards plashing and gurgling to the music of fountains, which rises magically on its hill crest against the backdrop of the Sierra Nevada. It was also the Moors' last stronghold in Spain, falling to the Catholic Monarchs Ferdinand and Isabella only in 1492 – the young Moorish king, Boabdil, is said to have 'wept like a woman' on handing over the keys of his beautiful city. This triumphant conclusion to the *Reconquista* was no unsullied triumph for Spain as a whole. The Catholic Monarchs, in spite of promises made to Boabdil,

Pine kernels, laboriously extracted from the cones, are an important crop. They are used in confectionery, above all as one of the ingredients in turrón, *the deliciously rich sweetmeat which comes in various forms (some similar to nougat) and is traditionally eaten at Christmas.*

The town of Ronda (opposite) presents scenes that might have emerged from the Middle Ages. Its position too is extremely dramatic: perched on a jagged rock rising 400 feet from the surrounding plain, with a deep gorge spanned by a fine 18th-century bridge separating its two halves.

Moorish, Christian and Jewish influences, combined with New World wealth from the imperial era, have made Seville one of Spain's most gracious and exuberant cities. All major architectural styles are represented, from Gothic and mudéjar *(the distinctive style of Moorish-trained craftsmen working for Christian masters) to Baroque. The city is a network of mostly narrow streets, lined with low, white houses and palaces, and festooned with wrought-iron balconies and dazzling displays of potted flowers.*

proceeded to expel both Jews and Muslims from their realms, thus robbing Andalucía of its intellectual elite, its best philosophers, doctors and agricultural experts. The region was parcelled out in feudal fiefdoms to the Monarchs' land-hungry followers, who then let their estates and the sophisticated irrigation systems devised by the Moors fall into decay.

Córdoba was another victim. Under the Umayyad dynasty, originating in Damascus and reigning in Córdoba from 756, it produced the finest flowering of Spain's Moorish civilisation. Notable figures included the philosopher, physicist, mathematician and doctor Averroes and the Jewish philosopher and scholar Maimonides. The first Umayyad Caliph, Abd ar-Rahman I, started the Mezquita, intending that it should become the greatest mosque outside Mecca. Later, the victorious Christians cut a swathe through its forest of 850 columns to construct their own Gothic cathedral in the centre. The Emperor Charles V, grandson of Ferdinand and Isabella, is said to have wept, like Boabdil, on discovering this sacrilege: 'If I had known what you wanted to do, you wouldn't have done it; for what you have made can be found everywhere, while what you had before could not be found anywhere.'

Seville, the last of the Andalucian trio, is the one on which the character of Christian Spain is most firmly stamped. It too was the centre of a Moorish kingdom, of which the famous Giralda tower, once a minaret, is a relic. But its most prosperous years came later when it was the port on the navigable Guadalquivir from which the expeditions for the New World were mounted, and to which much of the wealth found there returned. Even so, it also reveals strong traces of the Moorish influence – in, for example, the shady, whitewashed patios of the Casa de Pilatos, completed in 1540 for a local nobleman. There is a touch, too, of oriental extravagance in the extraordinary outpourings of its two great *fiestas:* the processions of Holy Week (*Semana Santa*) and the bullfights and horse parades of the April *Feria* (Fair).

Death in the afternoon

If the Moorish influence is one key to Andalucía, the town of Ronda perched impressively on a crag in the western part of Málaga province provides another. In Victorian times it was popular with the British who used to retreat there from Gibraltar to escape the summer heat. But for Spanish people its importance is quite different. For them, it is the town that boasts the largest bullring in Spain and the headquarters of the art of *toreo* (bullfighting). Here, in 1785, a group of local notables set up the *Maestranza,* the body which lay down the classic rules of bullfighting and took charge of enforcing them. In the same century, the legendary Pedro Romero, from a famous Ronda bullfighting dynasty and regarded as perhaps the greatest *torero* of

May 3 is Granada's Fiesta de las Cruces *(Festival of the Crosses). Everywhere people buy and sell flowers. Patios and streets are decorated with crosses made from flowers, and public monuments are wreathed with floral displays.*

all time, established a school of bullfighting in the town. It still exists, training some of the most elegant practitioners of the art (and woe betide any ignorant foreigner who suggests to a Spanish aficionado that bullfighting might be considered at best a sport rather than an art).

Another Andalucian bullfighting shrine is the drab city of Linares set among the mineral-rich hills of Jaén province in the north. The city itself has few charms – its claim to fame is that the great Manolete met his death there in 1947, aged just 30. He is still regarded as the 20th century's greatest *torero,* who used to say with jaunty pride: *Por eso cobro lo que cobro ... porque soy Manolete* ('For this reason, I earn what I earn ... because

The job of the peón *is to prepare the bull for the fight. He taunts it with the red cape, or* muleta, *thus focusing its attention on the garment as well as helping to tire it. The matador, meanwhile, is able to watch and gauge the creature's ferocity. Things are sometimes confused by a* espontáneo, *a member of the public who spontaneously leaps into the ring to have his part of the show.*

I'm Manolete'). The story of his last moments is dramatic in the extreme, and locals tell it and retell it with gruesome relish.

Manolete found himself facing a bull of exceptional ferocity and craftiness, and seemed to be showing rare signs of uncertainty. An enraged crowd, noticing this, let fly with a barrage of catcalls and whistles and started taunting him with the name of his deadly rival, the Mexican Carlos Arruza. Pale with wounded pride, Manolete hurled himself back into the fray, to be horribly gored by the bull, who tossed him in the air and then dropped him on the sand of the bullring. He was taken to the hospital where the best efforts of the surgeons were unable to save him. His last concern seems to have been for Islero, the bull. When told 'He is dead', Manolete himself died in peace ... or so the story goes. Outside the hospital, meanwhile, the same crowds

that had earlier booed him were mobbing the men of the Guardia Civil on duty there, to let them in so that they could take away some relic of their dead idol.

Don Quixote and Dulcinea

'In a certain village in La Mancha, which I do not wish to name, ...' begins the most famous work of Spanish literature, Miguel de Cervantes's *Don Quixote*. The high, undulating plateau of La Mancha, stretching north from the Sierra Morena on the frontier with Andalucía, is the central Spanish landscape at its most austere and yet appealing in a bleak way – a fitting setting for the antics of Cervantes's nobly mad hero. It is above all a dry land – its name comes from the Arabic *manxa*, 'parched earth' – but the use of irrigation has made it

highly productive. On all sides, olive groves, vineyards and wheat fields, interspersed with copses of cork oaks and rough pastures grazed by sheep, sweep in low waves to the horizon, while overhead the sky is a play of brilliant, clear blues. In summer the heat is suffocating; at other times of the year, bitter winds lash the plateau.

Cervantes knew La Mancha from his years as an official responsible for gathering provisions for the Spanish Armada sent against Elizabethan England in 1588. Until then his career had been distinctly uneven – including a spell as a soldier, being captured by Algerian pirates and spending five years as the slave of a Greek merchant in Algiers – and it was to continue that way. He regularly succeeded in falling foul of the authorities, both local and national, and spent regular periods in prison. One story has it that he conceived the idea for his hero in the Manchego village of Argamasilla where the locals had indignantly locked him up after he had attempted to requisition part of their crops in the course of his duties. Certainly he states in his prologue to *Don Quixote:* 'I have been unable to transgress the order of nature, by which like gives birth to like. And so, what could my sterile and ill-cultivated genius beget but the story of a lean, shrivelled, whimsical child, full of varied fancies that no one else has ever imagined – much like one engendered in prison, where every discomfort has its seat and every dismal sound its habitation?'

Whatever the truth of such stories, the people of La Mancha have been careful to preserve the landmarks of

Don Quixote's fantastic exploits. Around Campo de Criptana, for example, are some of the windmills at which he tilted, mistaking them for giants (they are also a reminder that La Mancha was settled after the *Reconquista* by immigrants from the Spanish Low Countries). Even more resonant of the Knight of the Sorrowful Countenance is El Toboso, a typically Manchego village of low, whitewashed houses contrasting with the red of the surrounding countryside. This was the home of the girl Dulcinea, in reality a swineherd, in Don Quixote's imagination his 'Sovereign and sublime lady'.

In the north of the region, the walled city of Toledo rests magnificently on a granite crag rising from a bend in the River Tagus. The strategic potential of the site has long been recognised: the Romans built a fort here, and the Visigoths made it their capital until they lost it to the Moors in 712. But its days of greatest glory came in the centuries following its reconquest by the Christians in 1085. A succession of Christian monarchs, notably Alfonso the Wise in the 13th century, continued the Moorish practice of religious tolerance, in spite of the

*Seville's Holy Week celebrations are quite extraordinary in their combination of fervour and showmanship. More than 50 religious fraternities (*confradías*) process along different routes from the Plaza de la Campana to the cathedral. Each carries on its shoulders a sculpted* paso, *or float, richly ornamented with silver wreaths of flowers and bearing one of the city's many religious images. The crowds, meanwhile, address passionate* saetas, *hymns to the Virgin and crucified Christ, at the passing float.*

The confradías *are extremely hierarchical organisations which originated as medieval trades guilds and now involve a high degree of social snobbery. The members wear the strange hooded costumes of penitents, or* nazarenos, *and some carry lighted candles.*

The feria *(fair) reaches its most extravagant limits in Andalucía, though it is not confined to the region. With its roots in medieval livestock fairs, it is now more an excuse for several days of dancing, feasting and bullfighting. Parades of horse riders are another feature. The* ferias *of Seville and the port of Algeciras, opposite Gibraltar, are the most famous.*

Casares, spreading over two sides of a steep hill not far from Gibraltar, is the picture of an Andalucían village. Whitewashed houses and narrow, cobbled streets climb the hill, which is topped by a ruined castle, while a deep tajo (gorge) cuts the village off to the west. Hens, dogs and the occasional donkey or pig wander the streets, as women in black go about their chores.

Some of the windmills that Don Quixote mistook for giants still stud the landscape around the villages of Mota del Cuervo and Campo de Criptana in La Mancha. It is a flat and strangely beautiful region. The dry, sunny climate creates glorious effects of light, in which the white of villages, the rich colours of decorative tiles, and the yellow fields of wheat stretching out as far as the eye can see, are picked out with a dazzling brilliance.

Land of the Conquistadores

Extremadura, lying between La Mancha and Portugal, is one of Spain's poorest regions. It is also one of its most backward, where aristocratic landowners still own huge semi-feudal domains or *latifundios,* many well over 12,000 acres in extent. Cattle, pigs and black *toros bravos* (fighting bulls) graze its pasturelands, which are dotted with oak groves. In the Middle Ages shepherds and cowherds from neighbouring regions used to bring their flocks and herds here in winter to feed on the *extremos,* or winter pastures, from which the region gets its name.

Emigration has always been part of the pattern of life in Extremadura – in the old days to the Americas, nowadays to the most prosperous regions of Spain. Above all, it was the birthplace of most of the Conquistadores, the undeniably intrepid, but equally ruthless and often cruel, conquerors of the New World – hence the number of Latin American towns and cities with Extremaduran names: Plasencia, Medellín, Mérida, Trujillo. Francisco Pizarro, who by guile, treachery and amazing courage conquered the Inca empire, was born at Trujillo, and is commemorated with a superb equestrian statue in its main square.

One of his townsmen was Francisco de Orellana, explorer of the Amazon. The conqueror of Guatemala, Pedro de Alvarado, came from Badajoz. Jerez de los Caballeros was the birthplace of Hernando de Soto, the first European to discover the Mississippi, and of Vasco Núñez de Balboa, the first European to discover the Pacific. Hernán Cortés, conqueror of Mexico and (like all the others) responsible for many massacres of Indians, came from Medellín. All returned from their travels laden with wealth and built themselves the sumptuous palaces that are still such a feature of Extremaduran towns.

The region also boasts Our Lady of Guadalupe,

Times are changing as Spain adapts increasingly to the ways of the rest of Europe, but the extended family holds its place at the centre of everyday life. Parents, grandparents and unmarried aunts and uncles still tend to live together, and children stay at home until they are married. Even in sophisticated centres such as Madrid and Barcelona, the unmarried girl who leaves home to set up on her own in a small flat is likely to be given a difficult time by the older members of her family.

efforts of the Catholic hierarchy to reverse it. The city's Jewish community flourished, often providing the kings' wisest counsellors, and a school of translators was set up. This had an incalculable effect not just on Spanish but on European scholarship, for its translators first made known in a European language many of the works of classical antiquity as well as of the scholars of the Islamic world. Sadly, the Catholic Monarchs reversed their predecessors' policy and Toledo went into decline as a seat of learning – though it was to have another bright spell in the 16th century when the Cretan artist Domenikos Theotokópoulos, better known as El Greco (The Greek), settled here. His strangely elongated works were somewhat puzzling to his patron King Philip II but were appreciated by the Toledans.

another of Spain's great Virgins, whose sanctuary is tucked into the scrubby southern slopes of the Sierra de Guadalupe. The devout have long regarded her as the patron of the Hispanic world (*Hispanidad*). Columbus came to Guadalupe each time he returned from one of his voyages to give thanks to the Virgin. She is Mexico's patron, and as recently as October 12, 1928, was officially proclaimed Queen of Hispanidad. Guadalupe is still an enchanting place. Clustering with a medieval quiet around the high ramparts of its monastery is a village of narrow streets and small squares which tinkle to the sound of fountains where donkeys and cattle come to drink. The monastery itself houses a cycle of sombre but powerful paintings of its most notable priors by the 17th-century painter Francisco de Zurbarán. It also has some fine Mudéjar architecture, the work of Moorish craftsmen employed by Christian masters.

North of the Sierra de Guadalupe, across the Tagus (Tajo) valley, rises the Sierra de Gredos, the mountain barrier that forms Extremadura's northern boundary. A narrow valley near its south-western tip shelters Yuste, the spot where the Holy Roman Emperor Charles V chose to retire in 1556. In this secluded place, the man who until then had been the most powerful in the world – heir through his mother Joan the Mad to the Spanish and American domains of Ferdinand and Isabella and through his father Philip the Fair to the Habsburg realms in central Europe and the Low Countries – spent the last two years of his life, plagued by gout but glad to have left behind the cares of his position. He lived in a handful of rooms, all decorated in his favourite colour, black, with a selection of his favourite paintings, among

them many of Titian's finest works. He was attended by some 50 servants including a master clockmaker, El Juanelo, who helped him to repair the clocks and mechanical devices he had collected during his lifetime. He knew his death was near and was determined to prepare for it – to the extent of planning his funeral and having it rehearsed before his eyes. When death finally came on September 21, 1558, his last words were a reminder of the long years of imperial responsibility, 'To rule is our business,' followed by a poignant, '*¡No hay remedio!*' – 'It can't be helped!'

Castile the noble and high-minded

For centuries, there have been two Castiles: Castilla la Vieja (Old Castile) in the north-west, the first part of the central Spanish plateau to be reconquered from the Moors; and Castilla la Nueva (New Castile) to the south-east. The root of the name is clear enough – it comes from the Latin *castella,* on account of the many castles that still rise, though now mostly in ruins, from hilltops across the region.

The landscape is not immediately attractive, though with an undoubted grandeur. In the words of the writer Miguel de Unamuno, it is a land of 'fiery expanses, uncovered and vast, without foliage and without streams'. Fawn-coloured countryside spreads out for miles, scattered with villages and towns where low houses stand out in the same shade of ochre yellow as the dusty roads and fields of wheat. The climate is harsh and extreme: droughts are a regular threat in summer; snows, late frosts and icy winds are a constant torment in winter. And yet this landscape has also been a recurring inspiration for many of Spain's greatest modern writers: the masters of the so-called Generation of 1898, including the essayists Azorín and Unamuno, the poet Antonio Machado and the philosopher José Ortega y Gasset; and contemporary writers such as the novelists Camilo José Cela (winner of the Nobel Prize for Literature in 1989) and Miguel Delibes. For them, it has always been a symbol of the old Castilian virtues of austerity and high-mindedness, the traditional scorn of wealth and resignation in the face of misfortune – as well perhaps as the less attractive Castilian quality of intolerance, especially in religious matters.

For long these characteristics seemed as unchangeable as the landscape itself. In fact, however, recent years have seen marked changes – in most ways for the better, though in some for the worse. The Spain of the 1990s, since 1986 a member of the European Community and ever more integrated in the mainstream of European life, is happily a very different place from the Spain of only 20 years ago – cut off from the rest of the continent by the Franco dictatorship. And yet some things have been lost. As more and more people flock to the cities and lose touch with their *pueblos* (villages), so they lose touch with much of the attractive simplicity of the old ways – they are now only too happy, for

Salamanca is 'the most beautiful, the most pleasant city in Castile, where nobility vies with beauty, letters with the arts of war' – so wrote the author María de Zayas. And her comment is scarcely an exaggeration. Its Plaza Mayor is one of the largest and finest in Spain, and its university – one of the oldest in Europe, founded in 1218 – has long drawn many of the country's best writers and thinkers, including Miguel de Unamuno who lived and lectured there. It was also the setting of many of the rascally exploits recounted in the anonymous 16th-century novel, Lazarillo de Tormes.

example, to flaunt their wealth (real or wished for) in smart cars and a showy pace of life.

But perhaps there was always an element of wishful thinking in Castilian high-mindedness. The ancient city of Burgos in the north of Old Castile has one of Spain's finest Gothic cathedrals, 'festooned and embroidered, chiselled in the smallest details like the stone of a ring', as the French traveller Théophile Gautier described it in the 19th century. It also has the tomb of the most famous Castilian hero of the *Reconquista* – Rodrigo Díaz de Vivar, better known as El Cid Campeador, his title coming from the Arabic *sidi,* 'lord', and the Spanish for 'champion'. In fact, El Cid's life was not entirely heroic. Though clearly courageous, he was an unscrupulous adventurer bent on seeking his own advantage, which usually meant fighting for the Christians against the Moors, but also on occasion meant fighting for the Moors against the Christians. These lapses, however, were long overlooked. He became the hero of the greatest work of medieval Spanish literature, *El Cantar del Mío Cid* (*The Song of the Cid*), and was for centuries held up as a model of rectitude and honour. Indeed, he was nearly canonised – but the memory of his heretical wish, inspired by Moorish traditions, to be buried with his horse Babieca put paid to that scheme.

Land of fine wines and foods

East of Burgos, the Castilian plateau rises to a series of short mountain ranges that line the southern banks of the Ebro river. They shelter Spain's most famous wine-producing area, La Rioja – a region that claims to have been producing wine long before the Romans introduced the vine to its 'upstart' French rival, Bordeaux. In fact, though Spain has often been overshadowed by France and Italy, it can boast as proud a wine-making tradition as many European countries. It has, for a start, more land given over to vineyards than any other country in the world – just under 4 million acres, as opposed to France's 2.7 million acres and Italy's 2.8 million. Admittedly, many of these mass-produce cheap table and cooking wines, but they also include some wines of world-class distinction: La Rioja's creamily oak-flavoured reds; the fruity whites and full-bodied reds of Penedès in Catalonia; the fragile, slightly sparkling whites of Ribeiro in Galicia; and occasional one-off gems, such as the inky red Vega Sicilia, produced on a few unpromising-looking acres in the heart of Old Castile.

Equally varied are the traditional foods and dishes. The love of seafood is one key to Spanish cooking. Village restaurants, even at the driest heart of Castile or Extremadura, will almost always offer a selection of *bacalao* (dried salt cod), *merluza* (hake), *bonito* (tuna) and *pulpo* (octopus). Sunday lunchtime in many homes throughout the country means *paella* – a ritual as much as a dish, involving painstaking preparation of all the numerous ingredients: rice, chicken, rabbit, pork, and

various seafoods such as squid, prawns and mussels, as well as several vegetables. For more everyday meals, pulses such as chickpeas (*garbanzos*) and different kinds of dried beans (*habas*) are an essential ingredient, especially in the rich peasant stews from the various regions: *fabada asturiana* (from Asturias), *cocido extremeño* (from Extremadura) and so on. Also essential in most of these is *chorizo,* the spicy Spanish sausage. The different regions and cities have, too, their more elaborate specialities, such as roast sucking pig (*cochinillo asado*) from Segovia in Castile.

As befits a Mediterranean country, the bar and café have a key role to play in daily life. For the working man, the day traditionally starts with the rich combination of strong coffee or chocolate, a small glass of treacly Spanish brandy and *churros* – sticky tubes of fried batter which are dunked into the coffee or chocolate. After a few hours' work, it will be time to

A Toledan craftsman applies the finishing touches of gold leaf to an armorial dish. His city has been a centre of the arts and crafts since the Middle Ages at least. The painter El Greco lived there for many years, creating some of his finest works, and it has been long known for its Fábrica de Armas *(Arms Factory) which now produces knives and razor blades rather than swords and arms.*

return to the bar – or *tasca, taberna, cervecería, mesón* or *bodega*. This time the workman and his fellows may have a *caña de cerveza* (a measure of draught lager-style beer) and a *tapa*. *Tapas* are one of the special pleasures of Spanish bars: small portions of a wide range of dishes, both hot and cold – seafood, olives (*aceitunas*), slices of *chorizo* or perhaps a portion of the cake-like Spanish potato omelette (*tortilla*).

In larger towns or cities, the café, meanwhile, is important as a meeting place, or somewhere to while away the time with a newspaper. If coffee is what you want, you can have it *solo* (black and strong), *cortado* (strong but with a little milk) or *con leche* (white). In summer, a popular drink is *horchata* – which usually has to be bought in a special streetside *horchatería*. This is a milky-looking drink with a tangy taste made from the groundnut *chufa*.

As throughout Europe, special delicacies and dishes go with the year's chief holidays and festivals, especially around Christmas and the New Year. At Christmas, friends traditionally give each other *cestas de Navidades* (Christmas hampers), with wine, various kinds of ham, sugared almonds and sweets made of marzipan. Another Christmas delicacy is *turrón*, which comes in different kinds: some like a hard nougat, others soft and sticky and made from almonds and honey. On New Year's Eve grapes are a crucial part of the celebrations; as the clock strikes midnight, you are supposed to swallow a grape for each of the 12 strokes – a near-impossible task. Later, January 6, *el día de los Reyes* ('the day of the Kings', or Epiphany) is when Spanish families exchange presents – rather than on Christmas Day – and eat the special Epiphany cake or *roscón*.

Just a few miles off the main roads, you find the age-old Spain of vast, empty spaces, shepherds and their flocks and hills crowned with the ruins of the castles that gave Castile its name.

The saint of the burning lands

The walled city of Avila, perched on a hilltop near the north-eastern end of the Sierra de Gredos, was the birthplace in 1515 of a truly heroic spirit. The touchingly frail St Teresa of Avila was almost single-handedly responsible for reforming Spanish monasticism in an age when the decadence of the Catholic church was driving people throughout Europe into the arms of Protestantism. At the age of about 21 she entered a Carmelite convent in Avila and for the next 25 years stayed there as a simple nun. But during that time she grew more and more dissatisfied with the laxity and hypocrisy of convent life, until finally she set her mind on founding a new convent of *Discalced* (literally, 'bare-footed') Carmelites. Braving considerable opposition, she established St Joseph's at Avila, and went on to travel indefatigably across Spain founding 17 more. She was also an inspiration to her contemporary St John of the Cross (one of Spain's most notable mystical poets) who followed her example by setting up similar foundations for men.

Though dogged by near constant ill-health, St Teresa had an extraordinary spiritual energy, inspired it seems by frequent mystical revelations of divine love. Her many writings describe these, in terms which often display a naively erotic element: 'I saw an angel near me, on the left-hand side, in a bodily form. He was not large, but small, very beautiful, his face so bright that he seemed to be one of the very highest of the angels who are all fire ... I saw in his hands a long dart of gold and, at its tip, there seemed to be some fire; and he seemed at times to put it in my heart and it penetrated as far as my entrails; when he withdrew the dart, it was as if he took my entrails with him, leaving me ablaze with a great love of God. The pain was so great that it made me cry out and yet so excessively sweet was this extreme pain that there was no question of wishing it to go or that the soul could be content with anything less than God.'

West and north of Avila, the ancient university city of Salamanca and the now rather grimy city of Valladolid,

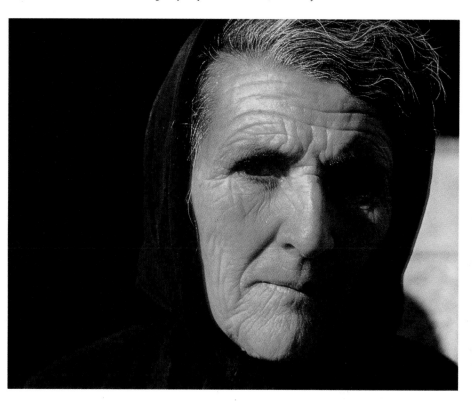

The lines of the hard life of the Castilian plateau are etched on the face of this old woman. All is extreme in this austere land – extremes of heat in summer, and of cold, icy winds and snow in winter.

The olive, the fruitful tree of barren lands, grows throughout the peninsula, except in Galicia and along the Cantabrian coast. Andalucía produces more than any other region, but the olives of Aragon and Catalonia in the north are considered superior in quality, thanks to the natural acidity of their soils.

Wild goats live in several remote, mountain regions across Spain, the three main breeds being those of the Pyrenees, the Sierra de Gredos and the mountains of the south-west. In the popular imagination, they are seen as a symbol of liberty and independence.

once the Catholic Monarchs' favourite seat, reveal the Castilian spirit in its more worldly aspect. Here are some of the finest examples of the baroque style known as *plateresco* (from *plata*, 'silver') inspired by the work of goldsmiths and silversmiths. The inspiration is clear in façades such as the entrance to the original university building in Salamanca, where the profusion of minutely wrought detail gives the impression of an elaborate piece of silverware transferred to stone.

The road striking south-east from Valladolid towards Madrid leads across the plain of Old Castile, past the city of Segovia (famous for its Roman aqueduct) and through the Sierra de Guadarrama, the mountain rampart that sweeps around to the north of the capital. Tucked into the sierra's southern tip is one of the stranger former royal residences in Europe, the monastery-palace of El Escorial. This was built between 1563 and 1584 under the close supervision of Charles V's son Philip II, the man who sent the Armada against England. Philip II at least had a truly Castilian austerity, and was determined that the palace should reflect his tastes. 'Above all do not forget what I have told you,' he informed his architect; 'simplicity in the construction, severity in the whole, nobility without arrogance, majesty without ostentation.' The resulting pile is certainly severe, though severity writ large – it boasts 1200 doors and 2600 windows.

A few miles to the north is another strange monument, the Valle de los Caídos (Valley of the Fallen). This was constructed under the orders of Franco to commemorate those who died during the Civil War, supposedly on both sides, though the labour came from political prisoners of the defeated Republican cause. Again austerity is the key note. A 400-foot cross rises from the mountain side, while underneath a huge and eerie basilica is carved into the bowels of the mountain,

Emigration is a constant bane of the drier regions of rural Spain. Old people are left to cope as best they can with family farms and smallholdings, while the young flee to Bilbao or Barcelona, or France or Germany.

Bread is literally the staff of life in Spain. Every region and many towns and cities have their own special kinds of loaf, and an intense rivalry exists between some neighbouring towns over the quality of their respective products. Bread made with maize flour is a speciality of Galicia as a whole, for example, but within the region there are the rye breads of Lugo and the loaves made from both wheat and rye flour of Santiago.

Saffron is an essential ingredient of many Spanish dishes, notably paella. It comes from the stamens of the crocus sativus, which is intensively cultivated around Valencia in the Levante.

Many Spanish towns specialise in colourful ceramics. Though much is now produced industrially, some potteries keep up the old traditions of hand throwing.

resembling nothing so much as a goblin hall from some fairy tale. Buried here, as well as the bodies of 40,000 Civil War soldiers, is that of Franco himself.

Heavenly city?

The people of Madrid, the *madrileños*, take a high view of their city's charms – '*De Madrid al cielo*' ('From Madrid to heaven'), they will frequently tell you. In fact, the Spanish capital – which only became the capital in 1561 when Philip II used a pair of compasses to find the exact centre of his kingdom – has little to compare with the concentration of fine monuments, parks and imposing streets of most of its European counterparts. Its greatest glory is the Prado, undoubtedly one of the world's greatest art galleries, with most of the finest works of Spain's glorious lineage of painters from anonymous medieval masters through Velázquez and El Greco to Goya. For the rest, Madrid has an attractive old quarter clustering round the Plaza Mayor, the wooded stretch of the Retiro park, the 18th-century Royal Palace poised dramatically on a low escarpment.

If there is any truth in the *madrileños'* claim, it lies in their city's social life. This has a formidable energy and, despite a growing tendency to conform to the patterns of the rest of Europe, keeps strictly to the traditional Spanish timetable. The afternoon siesta is inviolable – shops shut promptly at one o'clock and rarely open before four. The business of the evenings, by contrast, keeps going well into the early hours. Restaurants are still mostly empty at nine, beginning to fill by 10.30 and at their busiest as midnight approaches. After dinner young *madrileños* regularly head for discos and smart bars where they may stay until four or later. They then catch a few hours' sleep before emerging surprisingly alert in their places of work the following morning.

And yet, for all its architectural limitations, Madrid is still Spain's capital, and has been the scene of many of the most stirring events of the country's recent history. Here, the dying Franco was kept more or less artificially alive for several agonising days in November 1975 as his elderly lieutenants scrambled desperately to ensure a smooth transition of power. Here too, the young King Juan Carlos, whom Franco had groomed as his successor from an early age, disproved the hopes of the former *Caudillo* (Leader) by initiating the move to democracy. In Madrid's *Cortes* (Parliament) building, the fledgling democracy met its severest test in February 1981 when the Guardia Civil Colonel Tejero stormed it and held its now-elected occupants to ransom as part of an attempted right-wing coup. The failure of the coup proved a watershed. When the Socialist party won the general election the following year, many feared another, and perhaps successful, coup attempt. Plots were undoubtedly hatched by disgruntled right-wingers, but no coup ever materialised. Spain had achieved the remarkable, and almost unparalleled, feat of making the transition from dictatorship to democracy without any blood being shed.

Andalucía's flamenco is a product of curiously diverse influences – from the musical forms of the ancient Phoenicians and Carthaginians, Arab and Jewish music and even the Gregorian chant of the monasteries, whose droning melodic patterns have left a clear mark. But perhaps most important of all is the influence of the gypsies, who bring to the whole of Andalucían folklore the tragic sense of their long outcast race.

Portugal

Europe's westernmost country, embedded in the side of the high
and arid Iberian peninsula, is caught between two worlds.
Ties of culture and language bind it to the world of the
Mediterranean. But it faces the Atlantic, from which it draws
much of its vigour. The people are used to wide ocean horizons,
once dominated by the caravels of their great navigators.
And they still harbour a certain nostalgia for their days of
wealth and glory. There is a melancholy – *saudade,* they call it –
in their spirit, which is expressed in the mournful strains of the
fado and which forms an essential part of their charm.

Obidos, set within ochre-coloured walls on a hill above the coast north of Lisbon, is one of Portugal's loveliest small towns. Flowers peep from any available corner. And, everywhere, rise the imposing portals of ancient palaces and houses.

As in so many Latin countries, black is the colour not only of widowhood, but also of maturity, honest poverty and tradition. Older Portuguese women in some rural areas are distinguished by the way they wrap their faces in the double layer of a scarf with a hat perched on top.

Previous page:
Drying clothes create patterns of vivid colour against crisply whitewashed walls at Nazaré in central Portugal. The town has two lives: as a tourist centre and as a traditional fishing port. In the old fishing quarter, narrow, cobbled lanes such as this lead directly onto the beach.

Iberia's Atlantic Face

It was princes of French blood who carved out the modern state of Portugal. In the late 11th century the region known as Portucale – lying between the Minho and Douro rivers in the north, and named after the Roman ports of Portus and Cale at the mouth of the Douro – was part of the domains of King Alfonso VI of Castile and León. In 1097, he named the Frenchman Henry of Burgundy hereditary Count of Portucale as a reward for his help in the fight against the Moors, who then ruled large swathes of the Iberian peninsula. Henry's son Afonso Henriques, not content with the title of mere count, proclaimed himself king. He defeated forces sent against him by Alfonso VI's successors, and was formally recognised in his new title in 1143. He and his descendants then extended the new kingdom southwards until in 1249 they drove the last of the Moors from the southern province of the Algarve.

Although by geography so intimately connected with Spain, Portugal is quite different from its larger neighbour. Approaching it from Spain's stark, sun-baked plateaus, you are immediately struck by the softness of the Portuguese landscape and its greenness, which it owes to a damp Atlantic climate, especially in the mountainous north. The high ranges of the central Iberian peninsula fall to the sea in rolling hills, clothed with forests and pastures. Between them lie fertile valleys and in the south stretch rich agricultural plains.

Three great rivers flow across the country, forming its principal dividing lines. In the north, the Minho marks the frontier with north-west Spain. Farther south, the Douro (which began life as the Spanish Duero rising not far south of the Pyrenees and cutting across most of the breadth of the Iberian peninsula) separates northern from central Portugal. It reaches the sea near the country's second city, Oporto. The Douro valley is home to Portugal's most famous product, port wine, named after Oporto. To the south again is the Tagus (Tejo), another mighty river rising in eastern Spain and flowing into the Atlantic in the wide estuary on which Lisbon stands. Beneath its line lie the provinces of Alentejo (literally, 'beyond the Tagus') and the Algarve.

Land of gentle ways

As in landscape, so in character Portugal differs markedly from Spain. Unlike the proud and assertive Spanish, the Portuguese are an unassuming race who pride themselves on their *brandos costumes*, 'gentle ways'. Even their language is softer and more fluid than Castilian. It has been described as 'Spanish with the bones taken out'. The 'j' is not pronounced brutally in the throat in the Spanish manner, but from the front of the mouth with a gentler 'shushing' sound. The people are also extraordinarily welcoming. 'Portuguese politeness is delightful,' commented one 19th-century

English traveller, 'because it is by no means purely artificial, but flows in a great measure from a natural kindness of feeling.' It is a remark that many modern visitors to Portugal would echo.

In spite of some economic changes over the last few decades, Portugal remains a substantially peasant country – about 27 per cent of the work force is employed in agriculture – with the village or small town still at the centre of many people's lives. Portuguese villages, usually rising from slopes or crowning hilltops, are wonderful places, where life seems to follow age-old patterns. Whitewashed houses, roofed with brown or pink tiles, sparkle from the hillside. The villages are often encircled by well-preserved, ochre-coloured walls;

Beautifully embellished public fountains – or chafariz *– are one of the delights of Portuguese villages and towns. They were once a focal point of community life where villagers or townspeople met and chatted as they filled their water jars – they are still cherished by local people.*

pots of geraniums and begonias sprout from every windowsill and doorway in a maze of narrow streets and small squares; and, rising from the hilltop, there may be a medieval *castelo*. In larger towns a Gothic *sé*, or cathedral, is generally the dominant feature, while close by the *pelourinho* (pillory) may survive as a symbol of former royal justice. Coats of arms are blazoned around the entrances to noble mansions, and elsewhere are ornate fountains and flights of steps, their balustrades decorated with an extravagantly baroque splendour.

These glimpses of past grandeur abound in Portugal.

Women's liberation still has much to achieve in rural Portugal. On market day in small towns, you will see women from the surrounding countryside scurry around as they perform their chores. The men, meanwhile, mostly dressed in dark jackets and felt hats, stand in groups exchanging news and jokes.

For, though today it is one of the poorest countries in Western Europe, it was once among the richest, with the first of the European overseas empires. The driving force behind this great achievement was Prince Henry the Navigator, third son of João I and his much-loved English queen, Philippa of Lancaster, daughter of John of Gaunt. His country had the advantage that it faced directly onto the Atlantic, and so, eventually, to the riches of the New World. It was near to Africa, too.

During the first half of the 15th century Prince Henry organised and inspired numerous voyages of discovery down the West African coast and out into the Atlantic. The islands of Madeira and the Azores (still part of Portugal) were discovered in 1419 and 1427. By Henry's death in 1460 Portuguese navigators had reached the Cape Verde Islands and as far down the African coast as modern Sierra Leone. The impetus for exploration continued. In 1487 the navigator Bartolomeu Dias rounded Africa's southern tip, naming it Cabo da Boa Esperança, 'Cape of Good Hope'. Just over ten years later, in 1498, Vasco da Gama sailed round the Cape to reach India. Later, the Portuguese were the first Europeans to reach China and Japan by sea. They had trading posts at Goa in India, Malacca in modern Indonesia and Macau off the Chinese coast (the last still ruled from Portugal, though due to be returned to China in 1997), and by 1500 they had claimed Brazil.

These were remarkable times for Portugal. Within the space of 150 years, it had passed from being a relative backwater to being a world power with an unprecedented global reach. But these triumphs were to prove comparatively short-lived. In the first place, from the 1490s onwards, Portugal had a rival – its old enemy Spain. In January 1492, Ferdinand and Isabella of Spain drove the last of the Moors from their realms, leaving them free to pursue colonial ambitions as well. In October that year Columbus made his first landfall in the Americas. Two years later, the Pope brokered the Treaty of Tordesillas between Portugal and Spain, by which they split the world along a line running 370 leagues (over 1000 miles) west of the Cape Verde Islands – Portugal taking what lay to the east, Spain what lay to the west. This left Portugal with the Orient, seemingly the greater prize. But the truth was that Portugal had overextended itself and, by the end of the same century that had seen it at the height of its power, it had fallen under the dominion of Spain.

In 1640 the Portuguese seized back their freedom, and for a while there was something of a revival in the

country's fortunes. The discovery of gold and diamonds in Brazil brought new wealth in the late 17th and 18th centuries, and in the 18th century the autocratic reforming Prime Minister, the Marquis of Pombal, a former ambassador to London, had a measure of success in modernising the country. But it was a brief reprieve. The 19th century began with an invasion by Napoleonic armies, and continued with chronic political instability. It ended with the country near bankruptcy. In 1910 the last king, the diminutive book-lover Manuel II, was ousted and a republic was set up.

This did little to solve Portugal's problems. In the 16 years from 1910 there were no fewer than 45 changes of government, until in 1926 the army intervened. In 1928 a 39-year-old professor of economics, Dr António de Oliveira Salazar, was appointed with army backing as Finance Minister, then promoted to Prime Minister in 1932. Although never more than Prime Minister, Salazar would be Portugal's dictator for the next 36 years. He ruled with the help of a secret police force, the much-feared *Polícia Internacional e de Defesa do Estado* (PIDE). It has to be said in his favour that he

brought Portugal a measure of stability and, at first, of prosperity. But things began to unravel from the mid-1950s. The country became ever more divided between the strongly Catholic and conservative North and the radical South, where a large, landless peasantry expressed their discontent. At the same time, wars against nationalist movements in the remaining colonies in Asia and Africa – Goa (seized by India in 1961), Mozambique, Angola and Guinea-Bissau – were a constant drain on the country's resources.

In 1968 Salazar suffered permanent brain damage when a deck chair he was sitting on collapsed under him. His successor, Marcelo Caetano, introduced a few timid reforms, but on April 25, 1974, radical army officers ousted him in a bloodless coup – to the great joy of most Portuguese. People flocked to Lisbon in their thousands to celebrate. In fact, the country was in for another bout of political confusion. Stability only really emerged in the mid-1980s. In 1986 Portugal joined the European Community. The following year the right-of-centre Social Democrats became the first party since the revolution to win a proper majority in parliament.

A peasant woman sells her produce at the market of the local town. Life is hard for most Portuguese peasants, despite European Community subsidies in recent years. Even in some fertile regions, peasants scratch a meagre living from family plots of land that have been endlessly divided and subdivided over the generations.

A mountain chill hangs over Castelo de Vide in the Upper Alentejo region close to the Spanish border. The Romans first built a fort here and the remains of a castle and town walls testify to its later importance as a frontier post. It is also well known as a spa, its thermal springs emerging in fountains scattered throughout the town.

The mountainous province of Beira Alta (Upper Beira) is one of the most barren and untouched parts of Portugal, a place of granite, scrubland and some forest, where farming methods are primitive and rewards few. It was once the heartland of the Celtic Lusitani tribes, who under the leadership of Portugal's first great hero, the chieftain Viriatus, kept the Romans at bay for some 50 years during the 1st century BC.

The cradle of the nation

The lower Douro valley, centred on Oporto (Porto) and the heart of the original Portucale, is one of Portugal's most heavily populated and industrialised regions. Hydroelectric power is generated by dams on the Douro and its multitude of tributaries, and the range of goods produced, mostly in Oporto or Leixões which runs into it to the west, includes textiles, silk, tyres, chemicals, metals, electrical equipment, car parts, leather goods, shoes and soap.

Oporto itself is a fascinating city, proud of being Henry the Navigator's birthplace – though it is also a place that provokes mixed reactions. Certainly, its setting could hardly be more spectacular. Banks of red roofs rise steeply up the north side of a gorge near the mouth of the Douro, the heights above including an outcrop crowned by a 12th-century cathedral and bishop's palace. On the waterfront small coastal vessels are tied up, while far above, four magnificent bridges span the gorge. The city, though not over-endowed with fine architecture, has a few gems such as the church of

São Francisco which combines a Gothic exterior with a madly gilded baroque interior.

What can be distressing in Oporto is the contrast between wealth and poverty: on the one hand, the busy commercial centre and the villas set in large walled grounds of the smart hillside residential areas; on the other, the seething *ilhas,* the often filthy alleys which run off the dusty boulevards radiating across the city. And yet for all the squalid evidence of poverty, the people of Oporto seem to rub along happily enough. For the great *festas* (festivals) of St John in June and St Bartholomew in August – a love of festivals is a characteristic the Portuguese do share with the Spanish – they turn out in force to sing, dance and feast round bonfires on dishes such as roast kid. During the festival of St John they keep up the somewhat curious tradition of hitting each other with leeks. One of the centrepieces of the festival of St Bartholomew is the *Cortejo de Papel*, a procession for which they dress in paper costumes satirising politicians and public figures.

Oporto and the Douro valley are, of course, famous for the port wine trade – whose centre is Vila Nova de Gaia, opposite Oporto on the south side of the Douro gorge. The chief vine-growing areas are, in fact, well inland from Oporto and Vila Nova, starting at the town of Peso da Régua and stretching as far as the Spanish

The hard life of rural Portugal has etched the lines of care on the face of this young woman. In a land where the men often emigrate to find work in Europe's richer countries, the women have a key role in running family smallholdings.

frontier. This is a spectacular region where the Douro winds its way past steep slopes, on which generations of vineyard owners have patiently constructed thousands of narrow terraces. It appears at its most glorious in autumn when the rich purples of the ripe grapes and the russet tints of the leaves coat the landscape in a medley of colour. This is also the busiest time, the time of the *vindima* or grape harvest. The picked grapes are pressed on the spot, on the *quinta* (estate) or at a cooperative, and the wine is later transported down the valley to the 'lodges' of Vila Nova where it is left to age in huge oaken casks.

Visiting the lodges, you are ushered into the cool half-light of cellars gouged out of the rock and given samples of the different kinds of port: fruity ruby ports, made from blends of wines from different years, and aged in casks for a few years before being bottled; smoother tawnies, blends again, but left to age for up to 20 years; late-bottled vintage ports, made from the wine of just one year and aged for eight years or so; and the finest of all, vintage ports, made from the grapes of one exceptionally good year and aged for at least 15 years.

For centuries the port wine trade was dominated by the British, and one of its most sacred spots is still the Factory House of the British Association in Oporto, a gem of Georgian architecture designed by an 18th-century British consul and set on the street formerly known as the Rua dos Ingleses (Street of the English). The Association's members include, somewhat snobbishly, only firms that have been in the business since the 18th century, most of them with unmistakably British names: Cockburn Smithes; Croft; Taylor, Fladgate and Yeatman; Graham; Offley Forrester; and Sandeman. The British port families are still an important presence in the region around Oporto, living in splendid ancestral *quintas*. They are often now more Portuguese than British by blood, but still religiously send their children back to be educated at English public schools.

In fact, Britain has a long history of involvement in Portugal – it claims Portugal as its oldest ally. In 1386 the Portuguese, anxious for an ally to counterbalance Castile, concluded the Treaty of Windsor with England. The treaty has been confirmed many times since, most recently in 1899. Portugal's prosperity in the 16th century brought many British merchants to Oporto and Lisbon. In 1703 the Methuen Treaty allowed Portuguese wines into Britain on preferential terms, and resulted in the arrival of more British merchants, who came to establish a significant grip over the Portuguese economy. When the French invaded in 1807, the military side of the alliance came to the fore, with Britain sending troops under the future Duke of Wellington. From then until 1821 Portugal was effectively a British protectorate.

Northern fastnesses

The two provinces of Minho and Trás-os-Montes ('Beyond the Mountains'), lying to the north of the Douro, present a marked contrast: the Minho often known as the 'garden of Portugal', a fertile, rolling region fringed to the west by the Costa Verde; Trás-os-Montes, bleak and mountainous, where wolves are still hunted in winter. In neither province are the people rich. In the Minho, family holdings have been endlessly divided over the generations until many now cover less than five acres. As a result, every square inch of ground is treasured. Maize, beans, marrows and other vegetables grow at the feet of vines from whose grapes the Minho's distinctive *vinhos verdes* ('green wines')

are made – light, slightly sparkling, usually white wines. Cows – rarely more than two for every farm – graze in damp dells alongside the oxen that are indispensable for ploughing, reaping and pulling wooden-wheeled carts. Tractors and other modern farm machinery are rare, because the farmers are too poor to buy them and few have banded together into cooperatives.

The Minho is also the region where Portuguese folk traditions survive most strongly. Festivals abound, from the major landmarks of the church calendar to local *romarias* (pilgrimages) or saints' day festivities mostly held in summer. All are celebrated with dancing, feasting and processions in which local people carry elaborate floats. The ancient city of Viana do Castelo at the mouth of the Lima river on the Costa Verde has two

of the most famous *festas* – those of St Cristina and Our Lady of Suffering, both in August. The setting is superb. A medieval *castelo* dominates the city, whose streets are lined with houses sporting brightly painted wooden or wrought-iron balconies. There are fine 16th-century convents, beautiful gardens and at the ends of streets spectacular views over the Lima valley. For the *festas* people gather from throughout the region, all wearing traditional costumes in which red, black and white predominate – black felt hats, red scarves knotted around the neck, immaculately white shirts and black waistcoats and trousers for the men; red or black scarves or tumbling lace headdresses usually topped with a felt hat for the women, along with brightly coloured blouses, embroidered skirts and long white stockings.

Generations of wine-growers have put every available square inch of soil to good use on the steep, terraced slopes of the Upper Douro valley – the region that produces the grapes for port wine. The Upper Douro was the world's first wine-producing area to be officially demarcated – that is, reserved for special cultivation of the vines that produce genuine Vinho do Porto. In 1756 the Portuguese Prime Minister, later Marquis of Pombal, created the Company of the Wines of the Upper Douro in an attempt to improve the quality of the wines and to try to break the monopoly of British merchants based in Oporto. The region (since extended) within which grapes could be used for port wine was staked out by granite posts.

Viana do Castelo is just one among a constellation of fine towns in the Minho, all quite distinct in character, each with their own special *festas* and their own typical products. To the north, the town of Caminha, on the estuary of the Minho river facing the Spanish province of Galicia, is famous for its brassware. Farther inland, still on the banks of the Minho, is Monção, a spa town, also noted as the home of the best *vinhos verdes*, red as well as white. To the south, lying at the heart of the Minho, is the cathedral city of Braga (also an industrial centre), whose archbishops wielded immense influence in Portugal right up to the 1974 revolution. 'Braga prays, Oporto works and Lisbon plays', runs a Portuguese saying. Braga also boasts the Sanctuary of Bom Jesus do Monte, set on a wooded hill just outside the city, which echoes to the sound of fountains and streams. You can reach the Sanctuary in an ingenious lift operated by water power or by climbing an imposing baroque stairway.

West of Braga, the town of Barcelos has a popular market held on Thursdays. It is also famous for its earthenware cocks, now a tourist symbol for Portugal as a whole. They come in all sizes, painted black with red crests, fanned tails and decorated with patterns of yellow, blue and white. The legend behind them is that a medieval pilgrim passing through Barcelos was accused (wrongly) of robbery and condemned to death. He sought out the judge, who was just about to tuck into a meal of roast cock, and said, 'If I am innocent, may that cock get up and crow' ... which it did.

Moving east towards Trás-os-Montes, the countryside becomes wilder and more mountainous. Forests of pine, eucalyptus, oak and chestnut cover many of the slopes. Straddling the border between the Minho and Trás-os-Montes is the National Park of Peneda do Gerês, a region of deep gorges and serrated, granite mountain ridges. It has the last vestiges of the primeval forest that covered Portugal before history began and is a

The vindima *(grape harvest) at the end of September and in early October is a busy and cheerful time in the Douro valley. Grape-pickers gather from all over the region, working hard during the day and revelling at night. The steep slopes on which most of the vines grow mean that men still transport the grapes in baskets, weighing up to 12 stone when full, which they carry on their backs.*

Teams of shawled women drag ashore the fishing nets that are left to float off the coast at Nazaré. Once they have sorted the catch, which is often distinctly meagre, they take it to be auctioned at the fish market or sell it directly to customers in the clifftop part of the town known as Sítio. In fact, modern Nazaré lives more from tourism than fishing, and sights such as this seem to survive more for the benefit of visitors than for any profit that can be derived from the catch.

botanist's paradise – nearly 20 new plant species have been discovered in the Park. The land from here on east is only good for the raising of sheep; it is the most sparsely populated area in the country, with a few tiny hamlets scattered among the mountains, most of them living in near isolation when the snows fall in winter. Lying near the north-east corner is one of Trás-os-Montes's few sizable communities, the walled city of Bragança. The region around it is famous for its *Pauliteiros* (Stick) dances. Men armed with sticks and wearing red headdresses advance on one another and then retreat to the sound of bagpipes in ritual dances that were originally performed with bare swords.

Fishermen's coast

The Portuguese are a nation of fish-eaters – they claim to have more than 300 different ways of preparing cod alone. Fishing is the main activity all the way down the long, flat stretch of coastline that extends south from Oporto towards the Tagus estuary, interrupted only by the mouths of the Vouga and Mondego rivers and the bump of Cabo Carvoeiro. Fishing ports, often doubling as tourist resorts, stud the coast at regular intervals.

Aveiro, for example, lies among the complex waterways of the Vouga estuary. It has a key role in the fishing industry, its salt-pans providing the salt for fish-preserving: every day lorryloads of the precious commodity are carried north to the canning plants of Matosinhos. Drawn up on the beaches around Aveiro, you will see the long wooden boats with low sides and swan-like prows, known as *moliceiros*, which used to transport seaweed (*moliço*) – often employed as a fertiliser in Portugal. Interspersed among them are brightly painted *esguicho* fishing boats, shaped rather like gondolas with high prows and sterns.

South again lies the Costa da Prata (Silver Coast), a windswept expanse of coastline, where long sandy beaches backed by pine forests stretch as far as the eye can see. Figueira da Foz at the mouth of the Mondego river is Portugal's most important cod-fishing port. Farther south is Nazaré, whose fishing quarter has a picture-postcard prettiness much appreciated by tourists.

Its people, who have long formed something of a community apart, claim descent from the Phoenicians.

Inland, meanwhile, the coastal plain gives way to the hills and mountains of central Portugal, a region that is particularly rich in associations with the country's medieval past. In the pretty little town of Alcobaça, just a few miles south-east of Nazaré and famous for its earthenware pots, is the glorious Gothic Monastery of Santa Maria. This houses the tombs of two of Portugal's most star-crossed lovers, King Pedro I and his adored third wife and long-time mistress, Inês de Castro, the so-called 'Queen who reigned after death'. In 1355 she was executed by order of Pedro's father Afonso IV, who feared that she possessed an unwholesome grip on his son. On becoming king two years later, Pedro had her body exhumed and, according to legend, forced his nobles to do her homage. The recumbent marble figures now lie feet to feet – so that when they are raised from the dead on the last day, their first glances will be for one another.

North of Alcobaça, the towns of Aljubarrota and Batalha bring back memories from later in the same century. On August 14, 1385, João I, with a contingent of English archers in his army, won a great victory over a Castilian army at Aljubarrota. To honour a vow he had made before the battle, he built a monastery dedicated to the Virgin Mary at Batalha. This is another Gothic gem, housing the tombs of João, his wife Philippa of Lancaster and their children.

The ancient city of Coimbra, until 1255 Portugal's capital, lies on the banks of the Mondego inland from Figueira da Foz. It is famous for its university, one of the most ancient in Europe – founded originally in Lisbon in 1290 by the poet-king Dinis but moved to Coimbra in 1308. It was Dinis who did much to establish Portuguese as a language in its own right and to encourage the arts and learning in his realms. He also built Coimbra's somewhat fortress-like cathedral, the Sé Velha. Coimbra has another claim to fame – as one of the centres, with Lisbon, of Portuguese *fado*. These are plaintive, usually sentimental songs that have their roots in the music of African slaves working on the plantations of Brazil in the 18th century. In the old days, one of Coimbra's most picturesque sights was of black-caped students strolling the city's narrow cobbled streets and singing *fado* songs.

To the east of Coimbra, the summits of Portugal's highest mountain range, the Serra da Estrela, rise to 6532 feet and lead into the barren border province of Beira Alta (Upper Beira). In winter the Serra da Estrela

Except during local festivals, the women of Nazaré now rarely wear their traditional many-coloured skirts, worn over seven woollen petticoats. But for some of the older fishermen, the distinctive checked shirt is still part of everyday wear, together with the woollen stocking cap, or carapuço, which falls back over their shoulders. In the pocket formed by the cap's rear flap they carry their tobacco pouches, and sometimes their lighters and pipes.

High-prowed fishing boats, with an eye painted on either side at the bow, and propelled and steered with huge oars, are typical of Nazaré. At the end of a trip, they used to be heaved onto the beach by yoked oxen, though nowadays cranes or tractors are more commonly used. Fishing is still largely carried on in the traditional ways in Portugal. As recently as the 1980s, only 4000 boats from the country's 17,000-strong fishing fleet were motorised.

is a popular skiing area; in summer its slopes are baking hot. Guarda at its north-eastern end is an austere, walled mountain city, guarding – as its name suggests – the frontier with Spain. A chain of medieval citadels keeps watch over the strategically important valleys which lead into the neighbouring kingdom: Castelo Melhor, Castelo Rodrigo, Castelo Mendo, Belmonte, Almeida and Sabugal. To the south the land falls to the more open countryside of Beira Baixa, dotted with numerous chestnut trees. Here, the city of Castelo Branco has beautiful gardens and the local women make brightly coloured *colchas* or bedspreads, embroidered in silk.

The Portuguese, peasants from the interior as well as coastal dwellers, often carry things on their heads – perhaps a custom they brought back from their former African colonies. Here, a fish-seller carries his stock through the streets, ready to whip it off his head when anyone seems interested in buying.

Land of the bullfighters

The Tagus, flowing along the southern border of Beira Baixa, leads in turn to the province of Ribatejo ('banks of the Tagus'). Here the character of the landscape changes altogether, resembling rather the plains of the Alentejo to the south. It is a land of horses, rice-fields and huge estates or *quintas* covering thousands of acres. It is also, above all, the home of the *tourada*, Portuguese bullfighting. Every village has its *redondel* (bull ring) and every *quinta* raises fighting bulls, with the most spectacular fights taking place during the great fair at Santarém in June. The *tourada* is more elegant and less cruel than the Spanish *corrida*, in that the bull is not killed during the fight – the Marquis of Pombal is said to have forbidden this side of the entertainment after the death in a bullfight of a young man of noble birth.

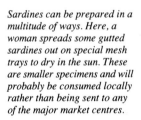

Sardines can be prepared in a multitude of ways. Here, a woman spreads some gutted sardines out on special mesh trays to dry in the sun. These are smaller specimens and will probably be consumed locally rather than being sent to any of the major market centres.

Sardines are abundant in the waters off Portugal, shoals of millions of them regularly feeding offshore. Fishermen go out after them more or less throughout the year, and the fish form one of the staples of the country's diet. Grilled over charcoal fires and slipped between hunks of bread, they provide a nourishing lunch for many workmen.

The people of Nazaré, with their distinctive costumes and fishing vessels, have long been something of a community apart, though in recent years tourism has done much to overwhelm their traditional way of life.

If the *tourada* represents one side of the Portuguese character, the white Basilica of Fátima in northern Ribatejo represents another. This marks the spot where, in the spring of 1916, an angel is said to have appeared to three young shepherd children – Jacinta and Francisco aged 7 and 9, and their cousin Lúcia aged 10. The next year it was the Virgin herself who appeared, on May 13. After that she reappeared in the branches of an oak tree on the 13th of every month. The children started talking about these strange happenings, but no one believed them – on the contrary, they were at one point arrested and thrown into prison. The anti-clerical government of the day accused the Catholic church of stirring up trouble, and even the church hierarchy itself refused to believe the stories. Nevertheless, the Virgin still kept on appearing, and Fátima began to draw its first pilgrims. These returned home with stories of astonishing miracles, leaving the whole country divided between those who believed and those who did not. Finally, in 1942, Pope Pius XIII claimed to have had a vision confirming the truth of the apparitions and officially recognised Our Lady of Fátima. Nowadays, hundreds of pilgrims regularly arrive at the nearest station some 14 miles away and make their way on foot across the hot plain to the Basilica.

Lisbon's fabled glories

Like Rome, Lisbon (Lisboa) is built on seven hills; like London it is a city of villages, a collection of *bairros,* or quarters, each with its own character, set down on the north shore of the Tagus estuary. Though no longer the fabled city of convents, spires and magnificent palaces

Huge trays of drying sardines give an impression of the sheer size of the hauls that can be brought in along the Portuguese coast – especially in the north. The sight is even more impressive when you bear in mind that the bulk of the catch is not dried at all but sent straight to canning factories, most notably those at Matosinhos on the coast near Oporto.

of the 16th century, it is still undoubtedly an attractive, animated place, made doubly appealing by the friendliness of its people.

The central part of Lisbon is the Baixa (Lower City). It was reconstructed by the Marquis of Pombal after the Great Earthquake of November 1, 1755, which destroyed huge swathes of the city within the space of five minutes. The Lower City extends inland from the waterside square, Praça do Comércio, in a grid of streets which offer fine perspectives and house most of the smartest shops and hotels. Rising on the heights to the east of the Baixa is the Castelo de São Jorge, parts of it dating from Moorish times, with the medieval quarter of the Alfama spreading over the slopes at its feet. This is an area of narrow lanes and tall houses, with washing hanging from the windows and pots of flowers and caged birds lining the balconies. It is also a favourite spot for friends to meet in the evening: they saunter through the lanes, dipping into the many bars, especially the *fado* bars where they can listen to professional or amateur singers or join in themselves.

West from the Baixa, a waterside road leads past another hillside quarter, the Bairro Alto where most of the best restaurants are congregated. The road passes under the Ponte 25 de Abril – the suspension bridge (renamed in honour of the 1974 revolution) – to the suburb of Belém, with two of the finest survivals of Lisbon's golden age, the Jerónimos Monastery and the Tower of Belém guarding the entrance to the Tagus. Both are richly festooned with decorative detail in the style known as Manueline, after King Manuel I.

Seafaring has always been part of Lisbon's history, with one legend ascribing its foundation to the Homeric wanderer Odysseus. Most historians, however, trace its foundation to Phoenician traders who set up a settlement here around 1200 BC. In 1147 King Afonso Henriques captured the city, and in 1255 Afonso III made it his capital in place of Coimbra.

Lisbon, and with it Portugal, reached the height of its fortunes during the reign of Manuel I ('the Fortunate')

Before railways were built along the length of the Douro valley, flat-bottomed barges known as rabelos *with a single square-rigged sail carried the precious barrels of port wine down the river to the warehouses of Oporto. Nowadays, sadly, the few of these picturesque craft that survive exist chiefly for the benefit of tourists.*

In Portugal, unlike Spain, the bull is not killed in touradas *(bullfights). First, the* cavaleiro *(in the old days someone of noble birth, and still often a major landowner) fights on horseback, using his equestrian skills to plant six* banderillas *or farpas in the bull's neck. Then eight* forcados *(traditionally,* the cavaleiro's *servants) enter the ring. They advance on the bull and the leader vaults over its sheathed horns to land holding on to its neck. His fellows leap on to the back, leaving one to grasp the tail. Once they have brought the bull to a halt, it is allowed to leave the ring in the reassuring company of tame bullocks.*

from 1495 to 1521, and his immediate successors. The tribute of Portugal's empire made the city one of the most dazzlingly magnificent in Europe. Its commercial importance drew merchants, bankers and royal emissaries from all over the world. The arts flourished too. Portuguese architects, influenced by the reported marvels of oriental buildings, developed the exuberant, late Gothic Manueline style, in its turn a key influence on the European baroque style. At the same time, writers such as the dramatist Gil Vicente and the soldier-poet Luís de Camões were producing some of the finest works of the country's literature, above all Camões's *Os Lusíadas*, an epic masterpiece, which celebrates the growth of the Portuguese empire.

Then came the long process of decline. The earthquake of 1755 – one of the worst ever recorded – effectively wiped out the Manueline buildings of Lisbon, with only the Alfama on its rocky outcrop surviving largely intact. It had a devastating effect, too, on the moral conscience of Europe as a whole, causing many believers to doubt the ultimate goodness of divine providence and prompting the French philosopher Voltaire to write his savage satire against facile optimism, *Candide*. Because the earthquake struck early on All Saints' Day, when many people were in church with the candles lit, the toll was especially high. Many who might otherwise have survived were crushed beneath the rubble of the churches; the candles started fires that completed the destruction. In all, 40,000 people died as a result of the earthquake and the subsequent famine and epidemics.

After the earthquake, the Marquis of Pombal set

Clad in black from his felt hat to his mesh shoes, an old worker stands patiently on a street corner in Lisbon. There is a large gap between rich and poor in Portugal: seen in the contrast between the smart residential areas of central Lisbon and the shanty towns (many without running water or sewers) that surround the capital and other cities.

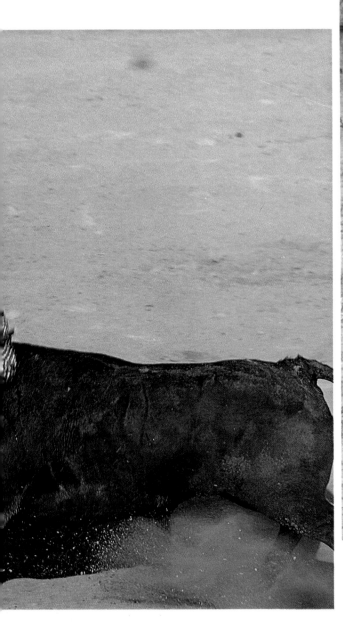

June is a busy month for Lisbon revellers, with the three Festas dos Santos Populares *(Festivals of the Popular Saints) to be enjoyed: the festivals of St Anthony on the 13th and 14th, St John the Baptist on the 23rd and 24th, and St Peter on the 28th and 29th. For these occasions each quarter organises processions, bonfires, street parties, dancing and singing. They are also celebrated on a more intimate scale. Here, a woman entertains family and friends with traditional* fado, *melancholy songs that often tell tales of unrequited love.*

Carnations have always been popular in Portugal, but since the Revolution of 1974 they have acquired a special significance – as an unofficial emblem of the new order. The bloodless events of 1974 are sometimes known as the 'Revolution of the Carnations', because they took place at the time of the year when carnations are in bloom.

Park benches provide an ideal setting for interminable Portuguese games of cards, played for pleasure rather than for the excitements of gambling. In the background a more bloody, medieval combat is portrayed in a frieze of Portuguese azulejos, *or tiles.*

about rebuilding the capital, but Portugal was no longer the great power it had once been and Lisbon never fully regained its former glory. For all its charm, its parks and public gardens, the city today faces many problems. Pollution from its industrial suburbs is bad, traffic congested, and many hillsides outside the city are covered with grim shanty towns. Since the revolution of 1974 Portugal as a whole, and Lisbon in particular, has had to cope with a huge influx of *retornados*: officials and traders returning from the freed colonies – although to some extent this has offset another endemic problem, emigration. For several decades now, there has been a constant outflow of young people seeking better prospects abroad, above all in France.

Royal refuges

West from Belém, Lisbon tails off into the stretch of coastline known as the Costa do Estoril, which is dotted with luxury resorts of a rather old-fashioned splendour such as Estoril. Inland and to the north is the glorious hill town of Sintra where the Portuguese kings had their summer palace, and where many of Europe's former crowned heads have now sought refuge. The poet Byron visited Sintra in 1809 and like many others was enchanted, describing it as uniting 'in itself the wildness of the Western Highlands with the verdure of the South of France'.

Portugal's largest province, the Alentejo, stretches south of Lisbon and the Tagus spreading across the width of the country from the Costa Dourada (Golden Coast) in the west to the Spanish border in the east. Olive trees and cork oaks cover its hillier, more barren parts, particularly in the north-east. On the southern

plains, around the ancient city of Beja, these give way to vast blankets of wheat. Like the Ribatejo, the Alentejo is a province of huge estates (*latifúndios*) – though after the 1974 revolution some of the *latifúndios* were expropriated and turned into farm cooperatives. Not surprisingly, it is one of the chief strongholds of Portugal's left-wing parties.

It is also a province of blindingly white villages and ancient hilltop towns and cities. Estremoz in the east (famous for its *bonecos*, gaudily painted earthenware figurines which depict peasants at work) was founded by the Romans and fortified in turn by the Moors and by Afonso III. It houses the Pousada da Rainha Santa Isabel, one of the chain of state-run hotels similar to Spain's *paradores*.

To the south-east, Évora (the Alentejo's capital) is one of Portugal's best-preserved citadel towns, declared a World Patrimony by UNESCO in 1986. It boasts no fewer than three sets of walls, the oldest – the Roman ones – dating in part from as early as the 1st century BC. Later, in the 14th to 16th centuries, Évora was a favourite royal residence and it is from then that most of its palaces, churches and convents date.

Moorish garden

It was the Moors who gave Portugal's southernmost province its name: the Algarve, from the Arabic *al-gharb*, 'garden'. And they named it well. Leaving the somewhat monotonous plains of the southern Alentejo behind, you enter a gentler, more rolling land carpeted in season with flowers and gloriously scented groves of oranges, lemons, olives, figs, carobs and grenadines. Snow rarely falls this far south, but in late January the

country is covered with a different kind of mantle – that of the white blossoms of its almond trees. The Algarve possesses another seductive charm, one that has made its fortune in recent decades as among Europe's most popular tourist centres: its brilliantly turquoise sea and long, golden strands of beach, backed by rocky bluffs or gently rising pine groves.

In many ways, of course, tourism has marred the beauty of the Algarve coast. It was once a place of small fishing communities, but it is now lined with luxury hotels, casinos, discos and golf courses. Even so, much remains to be enjoyed, and there are a few notable gems. One of these is the little chapel of São Lourenço, a few miles north-west of the Algarve's capital Faro.

The interior of the chapel, which dates from around 1730, is covered from the floor up to the dome entirely with blue *azulejos*, or ceramic tiles, which create astonishing effects of shimmering light. This decorative use of *azulejos* is typically Portuguese, a custom they acquired from the Moors. At first the tiles came in all colours, but as the fashion for them grew in the late 16th century, local craftsmen found themselves unable to keep pace with the demand, and people started importing blue tiles from Holland. Nowadays, few palaces, churches or public gardens are complete without their frescoes of *azulejos*, sometimes plain, but often illustrating the lives of saints, kings or heroes.

West along the coast from Almansil comes a gem of a different kind: the small fishing port of Albufeira, a place where tourism and fishing manage to coexist in a happy confusion. During the summer local fishermen go unconcernedly about their business among sunbathing English, Germans and Dutch. They beach their blue and green boats, touch up the paintwork, mend their nets, prepare their baits or tie together the curious earthenware pitchers they use to catch lobsters and crayfish. The town itself, which rises up the slopes behind the beach, is equally lovely. Houses are brightly painted with blue window frames and green doors – the colours of the boats – and adorned with balconies festooned with bougainvillea. In the narrow streets around the fish market, family-run restaurants offer seafood caught that morning: sardines, prawns, tuna,

small succulent soles, squid, *caldeirada* (a local fish and seafood stew), *ameijoas na cataplana* (clams stuffed with pork, ham and herbs), all washed down with a Lagoa or one of the Algarve's other aromatic wines.

The road farther west along the coast leads to the towns of Portimão and Lagos, with the Serra de Monchique rising behind and commanding fine views both south and west over the Atlantic. After Lagos the shore takes on a more rugged, windswept aspect as it bends south-west towards Sagres. Near here, Henry the Navigator established an observatory and school of navigation, which was responsible for perfecting the marine sextant and compass, whose manufacture was for a long time a more or less Portuguese monopoly.

A little farther on rise the desolate cliffs of Cape St Vincent (Cabo de São Vicente), Europe's far south-western tip, beaten on three sides by Atlantic waves. A legend tells how a ship bearing the remains of St Vincent, martyred under the Roman Emperor Diocletian in AD 304, was wrecked off the Cape in the 8th century, but that the remains were later rescued and escorted by a pair of ravens to Lisbon. Rather more certain is that several naval battles involving British fleets have been fought off the Cape, most notably the battle of 1797 in which a British force with the young Nelson serving in it defeated a Spanish fleet. Nowadays, Cape St Vincent is best known to seamen for its Fim do Mundo (End of the World) lighthouse which rises from the rocks where, as the Portuguese say, the continent ends in beauty.

Tears start in the eyes of a worshipper at the shrine of Portugal's patron, the Virgin of Fátima, which lies to the north of Lisbon. From the spring of 1917 the Virgin Mary is said to have appeared several times to three local shepherd children in the branches of an oak tree at Fátima. These apparitions caused great controversy at the time, but by 1967 they had been recognised as authentic by the Roman Catholic church. On May 13 that year – the anniversary of the first apparition – Pope Paul VI came to Portugal to consecrate a chapel built where the oak had once stood. Fátima is now the country's foremost centre of pilgrimage, millions gathering on the huge esplanade in front of the chapel on May 13 each year.

Yugoslavia

Loyalties as fierce as the landscape, and hatreds that stretch back
for centuries, may be destined to consign the very name of
Yugoslavia to the history books. As Croats, Slovenes, Bosnians
and other groups make their bids for independence, the fragile
unity of the Yugoslav Federation is cruelly exposed.
To understand the extraordinary variety of this collection of
peoples, cultures and landscapes is to understand why political
unity proved so hard to achieve and, once achieved, so terribly
difficult to maintain.

Fragmented Land of Beauty

The history of Yugoslavia is exceptionally complicated. Since the summer of 1991 the world has watched horrified as the land's two major national groups, the Serbs and Croats, have fought it out in one of the cruellest civil wars modern Europe has seen. But for centuries before that the region lying between the Danube and the Adriatic Sea has found itself all too closely involved in the rise and fall of overlapping kingdoms, empires and dynasties, movements of peoples, wave upon wave of invaders, and a kaleidoscopic process of combination, disintegration and recombination. The only way to understand it is to pull back from the bewildering detail of history and to look at the broadest possible picture.

The ancestors of the present population were Slavs, who arrived in the 6th and 7th centuries from beyond the Carpathian Mountains, supplanting the native Illyrians and Thracians. The Slavs were hunters, shepherds and fishermen, who grouped together in families – *zadrugas* – and clans. In the 9th century they were converted to Christianity, which penetrated their country from two opposing directions: from Rome, via the Adriatic coast, and from Byzantium through the Balkans to the south-east.

Croatia, which was converted to Christianity by the Franks, remains firmly Western. Serbia, on the other hand, fell more within the orbit of Byzantium and is decidedly Eastern. Both nations share the same ethnic origins, and practically the same language, but they are separated by religion. The Serbs belong mainly to the Orthodox church and tend to use the Cyrillic alphabet, invented by the 9th-century Macedonian monks Cyril and Methodius. The Croatians, meanwhile, are Catholics, and write their almost identical language in Latin script.

To add to the confusion there are Serbs living in Croatia (12 per cent of the population) and Croats living in Serbia (2 per cent). Some independent Slav states existed in the Middle Ages, though they did not survive for long. By the 16th century, the only town not in the hands of foreigners was Dubrovnik. The rest were controlled by Austria, Turkey, Hungary or Venice.

Resistance to foreign occupation was unrelenting. In the mountains of the south, peasant-warriors fought with great courage against the occupying Turks. In so doing they became figures of national legend. Yet each of the six Yugoslav nations – Serbs, Montenegrins, Croats, Slovenes, Macedonians and Bosnians – had their own forms of resistance, their own struggles to maintain a cultural identity.

Between 1878 and 1912 the Turks were driven out of Yugoslavia, and the only part of the country they retained was Macedonia. Then came the pistol shots in Sarajevo, in June 1914, killing the Austrian Crown Prince Franz Ferdinand and his wife Sophie. The assassination led to the Great War of 1914-18, and later to the creation of a single independent Kingdom of Serbs, Croats and Slovenes, whose name was changed in 1929 to a more manageable Yugoslavia.

This hotch-potch of peoples, later to become a federal socialist republic under Marshal Tito, held together until

Even in a backward region such as Bosnia, the sun brings a sparkle to life. But Bosnia has other claims to fame as well: it was here that the Bogomil heresy, based on a rejection of the material world, flourished in the 13th century.

In Sarajevo, capital of Bosnia, the unhurried rhythms of the East prevail. This is the most Turkish of Yugoslavian towns, where business comes to a standstill while coffee is served from little copper pots. It is drunk in the Turkish style, sweet, black and strong.

Previous page:
Lake Ohrid in Macedonia claims to have been the cradle of Slav culture in the Middle Ages. On its shores, in the town of Ohrid, the 10th-century Bishops Clement and Naum were generous patrons of the arts.

The distinctive triple-peaked profile of Triglav (the name means 'the three-headed') has become one of Slovenia's national emblems. The mountain, which is part of the Julian Alps in north-western Slovenia, is also the highest in Yugoslavia.

Albanian women chat in the primitive streets of Prizren in the province of Kosovo. Albanians form two-thirds of the population in the province.

Market day in Pristina, capital of Kosovo province, where the horse, the donkey and the ox still compete with tractors and cars.

his love of both liberty and tradition. Tito could almost have been a clan chief, but with a difference – he was a Communist.

Tito, a Croat, was born Josip Broz at Kumrovec near Zagreb in 1892, the seventh of 15 children in a poor family of peasants. At the age of 13, he became an apprentice locksmith, and later a metalworker and trade unionist. He was wounded and captured by the Russians in the First World War, and returned to Croatia in 1920 a Communist. For the next 15 years he was often in prison for his political activities, and adopted the pseudonym 'Tito' to confuse the police. In 1935 he moved to Moscow, and in 1937 was appointed secretary-general of the Communist Party of Yugoslavia. After the German invasion of Yugoslavia in April 1941, Tito organised and led a brilliant guerrilla campaign against the occupying forces. In doing so, he created a massive popular following. The royal government, which had fled to London, also had a resistance army of its own (the Chetniks), and claimed an equal share in any future government of a liberated Yugoslavia, but Tito outmanoeuvred and defeated them.

Having seen off the Germans and the Chetniks, Tito successfully defied Stalin's attempts to include Yugoslavia within the Soviet Bloc, despite a Russian economic blockade and military threats. When Stalin

the 1990s, when the strain of the various national rivalries, together with the example of nations seizing their freedom in Eastern Europe, started the process of fragmentation. First to break off were Slovenia and Croatia in the north, who declared their independence from the Yugoslav state in October 1991 and were recognised by the European Community in January 1992. Bosnia Herzegovina declared its independence after a referendum in February 1992 and Macedonia seemed set to follow suit. The Serbian-dominated federal authorities in Belgrade found themselves left with little more than Serbia itself and Montenegro.

The 'radiant future' of Communism

That Yugoslavia stayed together as long as it did was largely due to the leadership of one unusually forceful and determined man: Tito, a man typical of the nation in

died in 1953, the Soviet Union under Khrushchev formally recognised Yugoslavia's right to develop its own form of socialism.

Yugoslavia became the most open of the Communist states, and a leader of the international non-aligned movement. Through a mixture of capitalism and Communism in the economy, as well as decentralisation of political power, it was saved from the worst of the bureaucratic inefficiency, corruption, brutality and untruths that were the norm in other Communist countries of the period. While the Soviet Union and its satellites lived in the grim hope of a 'radiant future' which was constantly being postponed, the Yugoslavs,

Serbian houses, where the traditional welcome to visitors includes Turkish coffee, jam, plum brandy and a tray of cheese delicacies. Note the distinctive, high chimney stacks.

with their relative freedom, seemed already to have arrived, or at least to be on the way.

In fact, however, their future was to prove a risky and uncertain affair. The Yugoslav confederation managed to hold together for a decade after Tito's death in 1980 ... and then crumbled spectacularly. It became clear how much Tito's leadership had been responsible for keeping the state together.

Serbia – mosaic of nations

The territory of Yugoslavia is cut unevenly in two by the Dinaric Alps, running south-east from the Italian border to Greece and Albania, and widening like a wedge as it goes. The western portion faces Italy and the Adriatic, the eastern the Danube and the Balkans. Within these sectors there are several distinctive regions, each with its own peoples and customs.

Bordering on Hungary and Romania, the Serbian plains and the autonomous province of Vojvodina lie in an area that was once the site of the ancient sea of Pannonia and now has some of Yugoslavia's most fertile land. It is like a miniature mosaic containing numerous national groups, including ethnic Hungarians

A Turkish-style interior in Mostar, capital of Herzegovina. Notice the geometrical designs and bold colours of the carpets, the carved wooden cupboards, and the copper trays and jugs, all indicating a rich heritage of craftsmanship.

and Romanians. This is apparent from the range of traditional costumes. At Stara Pazova the women look like plump, happy dolls in their tight woollen embroidered waistcoats and full skirts. In Backi Manastir they dress in white lace, with colourfully embroidered aprons and heavy red necklaces. The ethnic Hungarian girls wear short skirts and red leather boots, while the Romanians prefer the more sober effects of rich embroideries.

You see this diversity in the houses, too. The Serbian houses in the Srem are white with thatched roofs and big covered terraces. In the Backa they build in brick, with baroque decorations on the façades. The Slovak

houses, green and white on the outside, and decorated with geometric designs, have clean and peaceful interiors, with painted wooden cupboards bearing the name of the mistress of the house; the cupboards are filled with beautifully embroidered linens all neatly arranged and smelling of sweet herbs. And the houses of the ethnic Romanians are quite different again: more crowded with furniture, heavy and massive. The plains themselves form a mosaic pattern, with fields of maize, sunflowers and peppers growing in the sandy soil of the Banat. The peppers are a speciality of the region between the Tisa river and the Romanian border and are known as 'red gold'.

Waterways dominate the two other sub-regions – the Backa, between the Danube and the Tisa, and the Srem, between the Danube and the Sava. The plains are crisscrossed with a network of canals, with dykes and locks. The marshlands of Obedska Bara are famous for their white geese and other wild birds as well as for their sinister shifting sands, which swallowed up whole battalions of soldiers in the two world wars.

There is a strong feeling of the past here. At Curug, in the Backa, a lone surviving windmill, now idle, returns the sky's empty gaze. A strange conical building turns out, on investigation, to be a hen house. The area is famous for breeding horses, for both racing and domestic use, and you still see people riding about in pony traps with traditional geometric designs painted on the sides. If you go up to one of the houses and knock on the door, you will as likely as not find an old man baking bread in an oven fuelled with dry maize stems. He will greet you courteously and invite you to sit down, and your visit will be honoured with a glass of *palinka,* the local apricot brandy.

In Ursac, ancient traditions survive in the carnival celebrations, when carts garlanded with vine leaves and bunches of grapes parade through the town. At Kovacica they have a tradition of naive painting – the peasants took to it, they say, because they used to get bored during the winter. Three of the best painters are women: Suzana Chalupova, with her pictures of rosy-cheeked children playing in the snow; and Marija Balan and Anujka Maran, Romanians who create enchanted tapestry-like scenes of country marriages with lovely, flower-decked brides.

Novi Sad, the capital of Vojvodina, is an industrial town which seems to sprout a new skyscraper every day: yet no one should leave the province without a visit to its old quarter, with its town hall, its Orthodox cathedral, and its masterwork of 18th-century military architecture, Petrovaradin Castle.

Kosovo is the other autonomous province of Serbia, and its population of 1.6 million is two-thirds Albanian, although there are also Serbs, Montenegrins and Turks. Foreign tourists rarely go there, despite its great forests of oak and beech, its spas, monasteries and splendid mountain scenery. The monasteries are relics of the Middle Ages when Kosovo was the heartland of the Serbian nation. The Albanians, who are Muslims, arrived only in the 17th and 18th centuries. As relative newcomers, they cling jealously to their traditional lifestyle. 'Jealously' is indeed the appropriate word, for you can tell an Albanian house by the wall that surrounds it, protecting the women inside from prying looks. Albanian women scarcely ever leave their homes and when they do, to go to a wedding, for example, they are an extraordinary sight: like walking jewels, wrapped in rich golden fabrics and airy silks decorated with flowers, and with their heads covered in veils.

Other images of the Kosovo plains stick with the traveller: the old narrow streets of Pristina and Prizren, their houses narrower at the base than at the roof, as if the builder had grown more confident as he went up; the mosques of Urosevac and Pristina, their minarets pointing like needles at the sky; and villages hidden

Novi Beograd, New Belgrade, positively bristles with skyscrapers. More pleasant to visit are Terazije, the centre of the city, at the crossroads of Zeleni Venac, and Republic Square – a lively and colourful place in summer with its numerous open-air cafés.

A journey through time

The Danube is more than a river; it is the cradle of several peoples. On its banks, at Lepenski Vir, statuettes were found in 1967 belonging to a previously unknown

deep in the mountains, their roofs so green with moss that you could almost plant gardens on them.

And so to Belgrade. The city has been destroyed and rebuilt no fewer than 38 times. It might seem rather churlish, therefore, to criticise it for lacking architectural interest, but that is unquestionably the case. Yet it would be a mistake to think of Belgrade as a city without character. It has a melancholy charm, which it does not reveal at first. You have to go looking for it. A good place to start is one of the artists' and writers' cafés in the Skadarlija district. There, you can drink beer and eat *cevapcice*, little pieces of mincemeat served with piles of sliced raw onion. Serbian songs are played, full of barely controlled emotion. When you have listened and drunk and eaten, the wistful, grey charm of the place will have got under your skin.

European civilisation which bridged the gap some 12,000 years ago between the Old Stone Age and the New Stone Age. The statuettes represented human heads, apparently in a state of terror at being born.

Travelling in this part of Serbia is like taking a journey through time. At the defile of the Iron Gates you can still see traces of a Greco-Roman road to Singidunum (Belgrade). At Balajinac you will be shown the head of a Byzantine Empress. At the monasteries of Studenica, Zica and Mileseva you will see stern-faced icons, angels with green faces and wings made of real feathers. There are ruined castles and monasteries everywhere. The towns alternate in style between Austrian baroque and modern socialist utopian.

Then there is the countryside. Agricultural machinery has started to appear, of course, but you still see wooden

Ottoman influence is clear in this home in Mostar, the capital of Herzegovina. You see it in the carved wooden tables, rich woven fabrics, and sweets dripping with honey.

ploughs pulled by teams of oxen and much farm work done by hand. Women dressed in traditional costumes of white with gold-coloured embroidery pile the cut wheat. This is their traditional role: the men reap; the women gather and bind. You will also hear the bagpipes played – a relic of the movement of the Celts through this land at the end of the 5th century BC.

At the markets, peasant women with white headscarves go shopping for the decorated clay pitchers where they store their water. A little farther on are the stalls selling *opanci,* the curly-toed shoes with soft leather soles that seem specially designed for creeping up on an enemy. Beyond them are the woodcarvers, who specialise in making miniature wells, complete with delicately chiselled roofs and wellheads.

Bogosav Zikovic is a Serbian woodcarver of European renown. The courtyard of his house in Leskovac is laid out as a museum of his work: tree trunks carved with scenes of war, fantastic beasts and folk heroes. The similarity to the totem art of the American Indians is remarkable, yet Zikovic is totally and authentically Serbian. If you visit him in Leskovac, the women of the household will insist on the Serbian tradition of hospitality and offer you a cup of Turkish coffee, a spoonful of jam, a tumbler of water, and a glass of *slivovitz* (plum brandy). They will also bring a tray of Serbian specialities made with cheese. The generosity is overwhelming, the quantities enormous.

The countryside offers its own, unconscious forms of art, in an endless array of rural images: the little water mill churning away by a stream; a frozen lake set like a precious stone in a hollow on Mount Sar; pagan rain

ceremonies by the banks of rivers in which girls are crowned with flowers; old women spinning wool and weaving ancient geometrical designs into carpets; a village festival where they dance the *kolo* across the newly springing grass. The *kolo*, incidentally, is a mysterious and very Slavic phenomenon: a round dance, performed with joined hands, which consists of three steps to the right and three steps to the left. The cumulative effect is a general movement to the right.

The painters of Croatia

After Serbia, Croatia is the second largest of the republics, now an independent state. Its population of 4.6 million is 75 per cent Croat, with a significant Serbian minority of 12 per cent – it was disputes over their rights that led to the outbreak of war in 1991.

The landscapes of Croatia are amazingly diverse: the Adriatic coast with its 1000-plus islands, which the brochures describe as 'the most deeply indented in the world'; the Pannonian plain; and the arid Karst region, which (to quote the brochures again) is known as the 'Croatian Sahara'. (The term *karst,* which occurs frequently in any description of Yugoslavia, refers to a bare limestone terrain deeply channelled and caverned by water, with underground rivers and, on the surface, occasional soil-filled hollows called *dolines*.)

Zagreb, the capital, retains some of its former Viennese splendour. From behind the ruched, ivory-

Yugoslavia is a paradise for hunters, and retains extensive wild areas of forest and mountains where every type of game can be found, from pheasants to wolves and brown bears.

Yugoslavia's gentler side: the green plains of Slovenia. The faces too are different, more Germanic and less obviously Balkan than in Croatia and Serbia and the other republics.

coloured curtains, you can almost hear the sound of waltzes, playing as they did in the days of the Austro-Hungarian Empire, before the fatal shots were fired in Sarajevo in 1914. With its neo-Gothic cathedral of Sveti Stjepan (St Stephen), its river (the Sava, which flows into the Danube at Belgrade) and its Western culture, Zagreb is a restless, intense, questioning place.

Are the Croats more like the Italians or like the Slavs? The truth seems to be that they are divided. While their coast looks out towards Italy, part of them remains resolutely Slav. The intelligentsia are cosmopolitan, but once you leave the city the Slav identity reasserts itself. In the countryside, you still see the Croatian national dress, with its red embroideries, and the Croatian *kolo* – a much franker, more open dance than its Serbian equivalent.

Hlebine, the home of the most celebrated school of naive painting in the world, is in Croatia, too. It was

A Macedonian woman in traditional costume, her lined face still showing the beauty she had in her youth.

founded in 1930 by Franjo Mraz and Ivan Generalic. The work is half primitive, half surrealist – rather like that of the French painter 'Douanier' Rousseau. Ivan Generalic, a painter of white stags in lunar forests and of bloody cockerels in the snow, taught the people of the village his art. His son Josip painted the joys of summer, great silver fish swimming in flower-banked rivers. Ivan Vecenaj was a darker, more tragic painter, while Kovacic is reminiscent of the Flemish painter Brueghel, although he is more intense and more wildly fantastic. A third generation of painters carries on the tradition, their work still labelled 'naive' – although, in fact, it is anything but naive.

Ottoman influences in Bosnia Herzegovina

In stark contrast to 'Austrian' Croatia, Bosnia Herzegovina is a land of unmistakably Turkish cast. It is all mountain: harsh, rugged and deeply folded. It is also one of the poorest of the southern Slav regions.

Bosnia's population of just over 4 million is 40 per cent Muslim, with 32 per cent Serbs and 18 per cent Croats. It is tempting, though wrong, to imagine that the Muslims have Turkish origins, for they are pure Slav and continue to speak their own version of Serbo-Croat. So where and when did Islam enter the picture? The answer lies in one of the great Christian heresies of the Middle Ages – Bogomilism, which taught that the world is controlled by Satan and must therefore be rejected. The Bogomils (named after their founder, Bogomil, a 10th-century Bulgarian priest) refused to accept authority – either that of the church or of the state. Like the Cathars in medieval France, they were extreme purists – too extreme, in fact, for the Pope and the Patriarchs of the Orthodox church, who persecuted them

Threshing near Lake Ohrid in Macedonia. The actions and postures are timeless. The wheat is beaten in order to shake out the grain from its husk, then tossed in the air to separate it from the straw.

The Montenegrins have a history of war. Shepherds formed clans, or katuns, *united by kinship and honour. This old horseman's splendid moustache comes straight from the heroic age – which lasted right up to the Second World War.*

mercilessly. Despite this persecution, the Bogomil faith flourished, spreading far into Europe and even reaching England. When the Turks invaded Bosnia in the early 15th century, they offered the Bogomils liberty to practise their faith provided they practised it under the banner of Islam rather than Christianity; the offer was accepted. The Bogomils left behind them a heroic image of stubborn revolt against everything and everyone – the last of them dying only 100 years ago. One tombstone attributed to them at Radmilija shows a knight waving an enormous hand as he leaves this troubled world. The image speaks directly across the centuries, as do the epitaphs on other tombstones, which suggest the depth and brutal clarity of Bogomil thought: 'Here lies Dragaj – in the end, nothing', for example, or 'As soon as I wanted to be, I ceased to be'.

Herzegovina takes its name from Herzeg (Duke) Stefan who led a group of Bosnians to found a kingdom of their own in the mountains of the south in the 13th century. Later, in the 15th century, Bosnia and Herzegovina became a single province under the Ottomans.

Bosnia Herzegovina was ravaged by the Germans and Italians in the Second World War. Roads, railways and mines were destroyed, together with 70 per cent of the province's industry. A quarter of the population was killed – a tragedy of which the many old women in black are a constant reminder. The people are proudly patriotic, sharp-witted, cunning, ironic, as well as fierce and dogged fighters.

Jajce, the old capital, is a quiet and pretty oriental town straddling the rivers Vrbas and Pliva. It was a centre of resistance to the Turks, the Austrians, and later the Germans. For a time Marshal Tito had his headquarters in the town, and it was here that Fitzroy Maclean, sent by Winston Churchill in September 1943 to report on the Yugoslav partisans, came to meet him.

Mostar is the capital of Herzegovina. Its bridge over the Neretva, the Stari Most, dates from 1566 and has a curious story. Its Turkish architect, Hajrudin (a pupil of the greatest of all Ottoman architects, Sinan) built a daringly wide, single-span bridge over the river, which collapsed. The Sultan angrily told him to build a new one, threatening to cut off his head if he failed. Hajrudin reluctantly tried again. The bridge was finished, the wooden supports removed, and to everyone's great relief it held. But Hajrudin was nowhere to be seen. The people of the town set out to search for him and eventually found him weeping as he dug his own grave. They carried him, scarcely believing his luck, to the Sultan, who congratulated him. The bridge still stands to this day: an outstanding feat of engineering.

Bosnia Herzegovina has plenty to offer the tourist. Apart from towns such as Sarajevo, Banja Luka, Travnik, Mostar and Jajce, there is much spectacular mountain scenery, good hunting, fishing, walking, climbing and canoeing.

It is worth staying for a while in Sarajevo, which is the capital of Bosnia Herzegovina as well as one of the most picturesque and historically resonant towns in the Balkans. Besides the more traditional visitors' sights, such as the charmingly ramshackle Bascarsija market in the old town and the great Husref Bey Mosque, you will find, in a street near the river, two footprints set in stone. These mark the spot where the Bosnian Serb Gavrilo Princip stood to shoot Franz Ferdinand in 1914, the incident which sparked off the First World War. In striking his blow for Bosnian independence against Austria, the young student could never have known that he was triggering a cataclysm which would engulf Europe and much of the rest of the world. Because of the war the Austro-Hungarian Empire collapsed, and an independent Yugoslavia was born. As a result, Princip is a hero in Sarajevo.

Montenegro – land of the black mountain

Montenegro ('Black Mountain'), or Crna Gora, or again Kara Dag, is the smallest of the republics. It is also the most dramatic in its contrasts. The subtropical climate and the relaxed atmosphere of the Adriatic coast stop abruptly at the mountains, giving way to a hinterland known as the 'sea of stone' or the 'lunar mountains'.

A Macedonian market at Struga, near Ohrid, where an international poetry festival is held every year in August.

The market in the Macedonian town of Ohrid provides a taste of Yugoslavia's variety of peoples and agricultural produce. The minaret in the background is a reminder of surviving Muslim groups.

A cheese merchant at the market in Belgrade. Little remains of old Belgrade, which was badly damaged in the Second World War, but in the markets you can still get a feel of Serbia's old patterns of life.

Traditional costume (right) on the Dalmatian island of Hvar. Notice the starched white headdress, which looks as if it might have come straight from a medieval painting.

Yugoslavia's different republics have rich crafts traditions. Among them, the lace and embroidery of Slovenia and Croatia are particularly renowned.

This is the Karst, arid and grey, where rivers have cut spectacular gorges such as the Tara Canyon (second only to the Grand Canyon in depth and length), its sheer walls rising over 3000 feet from the river bed. In the south of the country lies the most inaccessible mountain range in the Balkans, the Prokletije Massif, through which the frontier with Albania runs.

The weather is extreme. Montenegro is battered by winds and electric storms, and has the heaviest rainfall in Europe – over 180 inches a year – at Crkvice on Mount Orjen. The yugo wind, like the sirocco in Sicily, is so irritating that anyone who commits a crime while it is blowing can claim diminished responsibility. The snow reaches a consistent depth of 18 feet on Mount Durmitor during winter, and a number of towns remain virtually cut off from the outside world from October to February. Despite this, the Montenegrins manage to grow olives and vines.

Lake Skadar, in the centre of the Karst and shared between Montenegro and Albania, is rich in bird life, notably herons, black ibis and pelicans. It also produces a curious chestnut-like fruit, the *kasaronja,* which grows out of the water and is harvested by women in flat-

strict moral codes and a fanatical sense of honour, which sometimes resulted in vendettas – not just tit-for-tat killings, but a fully blown system of blood feuds that might well decimate families through several generations. They also regarded it as their historic mission to liberate their fellow Slavs, especially the Serbs, from Turkish domination. Right up to the Second World War, when there were terrible slaughters here by the Italians, the Montenegrins never lost their appetite for revenge.

Since they have always lived under the threat of invasion and destruction, the people of Montenegro have never built themselves fine houses or known the peasant's peaceful way of life. Their traditional homes are low stone huts, and even the royal palace at Cetinje, the old capital, is a simple and spartan place. But the Montenegrins have the looks, stature and bearing of kings and have always dressed magnificently and carried swords of exquisite workmanship.

Cetinje is set on a plateau high in forbidding mountains. Here, in the first half of the 19th century, the Prince-Bishop Peter I and his successor, the poet Njegos (Peter II), attempted to change the tribal structure of Montenegrin society and to introduce Western culture. They had a certain amount of success. Some of the trappings of the West were imported (including a billiard table which was hauled up the near-vertical mountainside from the coast by mule in 1830), but the graft did not fully take. It is only since the Second World War that Montenegro has begun to integrate itself with the modern world.

Traditions, though, remain strong. Weddings are

The father and grandfather of the owner of this shop both made ropes before him.

Opanci *are the traditional soft-soled, peasant shoes made of braided leather.*

bottomed boats. More conventional agriculture, meanwhile, is a matter of making the most of little: tiny patches of fertile soil amid the surrounding expanses of bare rock.

Life is hard here, but the Montenegrins are tremendous warriors, whom even the Turks never managed properly to quell. Their shepherd clans had

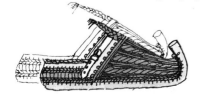

regarded not just as marriages of boy and girl but also of family and family. And even if the birth of a male child is no longer greeted with a salvo of pistols, and beliefs in werewolves and vampires have practically disappeared, the Montenegrins still play the *gusle*, a one-stringed fiddle, and sing songs of the heroes of the past with great intensity and longing.

A Slovenian couple in local costume. Yugoslavia is one of the few places in Europe where many people still wear traditional dress, even for everyday use.

A harvest of children

The history of Macedonia is as desolate as that of Montenegro and Bosnia. Its territory coincides broadly with the land ruled by Philip, the father of Alexander the Great, in the 4th century BC, but it has since been divided into three parts: one is the Yugoslav republic of Macedonia which, like most of the rest of the former federal state, is heading for independence; another, Aegean Macedonia, belongs to Greece; the third, Pirin Macedonia, is part of Bulgaria. Whereas most other Balkan peoples were liberated from the Turks in the 19th century, or at the latest in 1912, the Macedonians achieved independence only in 1945. This was a cruel irony for a people who had given the Slavs the Cyrillic alphabet, and had possessed, in the town of Ohrid, a brilliant centre of medieval civilisation.

The rule of the Ottomans was deeply resented. As throughout the empire, Macedonian children were taken or 'harvested' from their villages by the army, their mothers following them until they dropped from exhaustion. Many preferred to die by the roadside rather than return home, for their children were sent to be educated and enrolled in the Janissaries – crack troops who would later return to their native soil to fight their own brothers. Turkish harems, too, were filled with young Macedonian girls. Yet, bitter as these memories are, there are still Macedonian Muslims who keep their old customs and language, and retain a nostalgia for the 'good old days' of Turkish rule – rather like the *petchalbari*, the migrants to America who cling to a lost world, trying to re-create their old culture 4000 miles away across the Atlantic.

A great deal has happened to Macedonia in its 45 years of independence. Where there was once mass illiteracy, the Macedonians now have university professors, writers, a vigorous film and music industry and excellent theatre. In fact, they have achieved so much so quickly that it is as if they have been hurrying to catch up with lost time.

The historical and artistic wealth of Macedonia is dazzling: from the Roman mosaics at Heraclea Lincestis to the Byzantine frescoes in the churches of Ohrid; from the Jeni Mosque at Bitola, where the Turkish leader Kemal Ataturk used to come and meditate, to the Coloured Mosque of Tetovo. Skopje, extensively rebuilt after the earthquake of 1963, is filled with steelworks and skyscrapers, but retains its marvellous bazaar and artisans' quarter, the splendid Mustafa Pasha Mosque and Kursumli Han *caravanserai* – an inn for the use of large groups of merchants or other travellers. In its markets, engulfed by a sea of multicoloured fruit, you will see a wonderful variety of costumes: old Macedonian women in knee-length waistcoats, Turkish women in black velvet with white headscarves, gypsies in flowery gauze pantaloons, and veiled Albanians.

The Vardar river snakes through steep hills dotted with vineyards and villages baking in the heat. It passes the archaeological site of Stobi, an ancient Macedonian and Roman town ravaged by an earthquake in AD 518 (Stobi is sometimes called 'the Pompeii of Macedonia'). The river continues through poppy and rice fields to the tobacco town of Prilep, the site of the first Macedonian partisan attack in 1941. There, its waters are overlooked by the ruined castle of Marko Kraljevic, the hero of a great cycle of folk songs. Nearby is Tikves, the largest vineyard in Yugoslavia, and well worth visiting for its excellent and varied red and white wines.

Finally, the river reaches Ohrid, the great city on the lake where Slav culture first flourished under the patronage of Bishops Clement and Naum in the 10th century. A thousand years later, the town is once again a centre for the arts, with an international music festival and the Balkan folklore festival held here each summer. It is also a magnet to tourists for its beautiful position, its swimming, its hotels and cafés, its colourful market and its wealth of monuments and artistic treasures. In the neighbouring town of Struga, they hold a poetry festival every year – a moving spectacle in a land where free speech was strangled for so long.

The weapons of language

Slovenia, in the north, is the most Germanic of the republics. With its peaceful, green and orderly landscape and its neat red-roofed houses with flowers at every window, it is easy to see that both history and nature have generally been kinder here than in the neighbouring republics: that there has been comparatively little demand for the services of the moustachioed brigand hero.

They have another kind of hero in Slovenia – the type who fights with words, not bullets. The Slovenian heroes are poets who fought for their country's independence against cultural colonisation. In Ljubljana and Kranj there are statues to Francé Presern, the great Slovene poet who lived from 1800 to 1849. This romantic-looking man, with pale complexion and lazily knotted cravat, could easily have written in German. He chose instead to write in Slovene, and his love story *Baptism by the Savica* has become a kind of national poem of Slovenia, giving the language and the people who speak it a lasting cultural monument. Of course there have been bloody battles in Slovenia, too. The Second World War left its terrible mark on the village of Stermets, where the Nazis killed every male

inhabitant, including infants, in 1943. The women in black are still there, remembering.

The landscape of Slovenia embraces both mountains and plains. The gorges and narrow valleys of the Soca, the Sava, the Sora, the Kokra and the Savinjo rivers are thickly forested. In the south, a region of *karst* produces a haunting, lunar landscape and some strange seasonal effects. Lake Tserknitsa, for instance, is dry for half the year, and its bed cultivated as fields by the peasants. Rivers disappear underground and connect with other rivers before emerging miles away, only to disappear again into the rock. Some never resurface on land.

An underground journey through this region would be exhilarating, if impossible. To set the imagination going, however, visit the caves of Postojna and Skocjan. Here, in a subterranean world of sparkling stone and water, you seem to be entering a dream, a bizarre and monstrous fairyland of incredible shapes and structures.

There is no less drama above ground – at the two castles of Kamnik, for example, which are said to be haunted at night by a serpent woman with scales that glitter in the moonlight. There is also supposed to be a great mammoth which comes down to drink from the lake. By day, though, Kamnik is a delightful and popular mountain resort.

Evening in Dubrovnik, a city which has always taken the quality of public life seriously. The citizens had a state health service as early as the 14th century, and were ahead of many other cities in banning cars from the old town in the 20th. Tragically, the city was severely damaged during the fighting of 1991.

There are many other pleasant journeys to take in Slovenia through the hills and vineyards of the Krka valley or across the plains of the Sava and Mura. You should also find time for the towns, not least Ljubljana, an elegant, refined and courteous place where the streets are kept scrupulously clean.

Coastal drama on the Adriatic shore

Without the sea, the people of Yugoslavia would be rougher and grimmer, lacking that carefree southern gaiety that is liable to break out at any time. Most of

them never knew the sea before socialism brought progress and paid holidays, but these days the seaside is no longer a distant paradise for the Serbian worker or the Macedonian clerk. In summer, the beaches are crowded, noisy, friendly and, in many places (since they have freed themselves of the prudery of both East and West) naked.

Pleasant and lively as the people are, the real wonders of the coast are the landscape that descends steeply to the shore and the towns dotted along it, where the Romans and the Venetians left their distinctive marks. The beauty of these places should not obscure the fact that the Venetians were as invasive as the Turks, as exploitative socially and commercially, and far more interfering in matters of religion – to the extent that Ottoman rule was often preferred. Yet the Venetians left behind them an incomparable architectural legacy, which is one of the marvels of the region and, indeed, of the whole Mediterranean.

In the far north of the coast, next to Italy, lie the Istrian peninsula, Pula and Rijeka. These all have a mixed Italian and Austrian air, with the tired pomp of Riviera resorts in the 1890s. It is a world where a penniless Hungarian or Romanian countess in search of a millionaire would not seem out of place. This strange, wistful yet comfortable feeling of faded majesty also hangs over one or two of the Kvarner Islands; others, such as Susak, Cres, Kriza and Losinj – the breeding grounds of the great Dalmatian mariners – have a much hardier character.

Just south of Rijeka is the island of Krk (pronounced 'kirk') with its Romanesque church and its tiny fields surrounded with stones to fend off the winds. Then comes Rab, with its red roofs and white stone towers. Beyond lies an almost endless succession of islands and islets,

The Macedonians' folk music is as intricately patterned as the needlework on their shirts and waistcoats. It is meant for dancing, and varies in mood from the slow and melancholy to the joyous and bubbling.

A wedding in the western Macedonian village of Galicnik. Weddings here traditionally take place in July, and involve many ancient rituals. Notice the fine costumes of the guests as well as of the bride.

Dancers from Istria, in the north-west. The costumes here are plainer than those in the south; note the woman's long, pleated skirt, which moves beautifully to the lively rhythm of the music.

A guest at a wedding in Galicnik, loaded with silver and gold embroidery and wearing elaborate belts and a cummerbund with natural and relaxed grace.

all carefully terraced and planted with vines. There are the coastal towns too: Zadar, with its churches and its Roman forum which was discovered after a Second World War air raid, and the medieval streets of Trogir.

Korcula was originally an ancient Greek colony, and it may also have been the birthplace, in 1254, of Marco Polo – the honour is disputed with Venice. The Venetians took the island that same year, and the lion of St Mark still stands guard over the main gate of Korcula town – wings spread, Bible open at its feet, and mouth gaping in perpetual readiness to roar.

The Venetians first showed an interest in this coast in AD 997, and fought for control of it with the Croatian and Croatian-Hungarian kings for the next 300 years. They finally prevailed in 1301, and stayed there more or less continuously until the collapse of their own republic in 1797. Dalmatia then passed into Austrian hands, where it remained, except for a brief French interlude of 1805-15, until 1918.

Korcula is neither East nor West but, rather, a perfect marriage of the two. The town is a collection of beautiful Venetian buildings, with loggias and staircases decorated with pots of oleander, and a sparkle of sea glimmering at the end of every street. If you are there in the tourist season you can watch the island's traditional spectacle, the *moreska:* a stylised but highly physical enactment of a battle between Moors and Turks for a young girl.

From Korcula, as from most of the other island towns, you can catch a boat to Dubrovnik. This extraordinary city was recently (1991) shelled heavily by Serbian and Yugoslav federal forces in an act of war which horrified the whole world. On top of the human suffering involved, the devastation of Dubrovnik was a cultural tragedy, for the city is second only to Venice in the Adriatic for its concentration of artistic and architectural treasures. It reached a peak of prosperity from the 14th to the 16th centuries as a commercial intermediary between the Ottoman Empire and the rest of the Mediterranean. It was known then as Ragusa, a name from which the English word argosy, meaning a rich fleet, was coined. The membership of Ragusa's governing council was aristocratic though curiously liberal: they abolished slavery in 1418, established a public health service in 1301, Europe's first pharmacy in 1317, a refuge for the old in 1347, and an orphanage in 1432. At the same time they built themselves an outstandingly beautiful city and retained their independence from both Venice and the Turks. In 1667 the city was destroyed by an earthquake and rebuilt. By then, however, the focus of world trade had shifted to the Atlantic and, along with its rival Venice, Ragusa went into decline. Periods of French, then Austrian rule followed, until 1918, when the name changed to Dubrovnik and the city became part of Yugoslavia.

Farther south, the coast leaves Croatia and comes to Herzeg Novi in Montenegro. In this hillside town, set spectacularly at the entrance to the Gulf of Kotor, the atmosphere changes again: the air is more langorous, more perfumed, and there is an oriental indolence in the bearing of the young men. They sit, black-eyed and handsome, drinking coffee under the palms. We are back, in other words, where we started: on the frontier between East and West.

The Adriatic town of Korcula off whose coast a great sea battle between Venice and Genoa was fought in 1298. There is some debate as to whether Marco Polo was a native of Korcula, but it is known that he was captured here by the Genoese during the battle.

Greece

Few countries have a more awesome heritage to live up to than
Greece – birthplace of Western civilisation, of the arts and of
democracy. Modern Greece abounds in tokens of the glories of
the past, from ruined temples and groves dedicated to the ancient
gods to a language based on the tongue of Homer. It is also a land
of stunning physical beauty and astonishing contrasts, of snow-
capped peaks, sun-baked mountain slopes and idyllic islands set
in brilliant seas. It is a land where centuries-old traditions live on
in colourful religious festivals, intoxicating dances and music and
ancient superstitions, such as the fear of the Evil Eye.

Haunts of the Ancient Gods

The territory of Greece, which covers some 50,000 square miles, is made up of more or less equal parts of mountains and sea. Only 20 per cent of the land is level. Of the rest, some has been cut into terraces to grow olives and vines, some is used for pasture, but most of the landscape consists of a series of picturesque obstacles to the projects of man.

The mountains are limestone, which is hard but porous, and gives poor, thin soil that requires irrigation if it is to be of any agricultural use. It is here that Apollo, the sun-god, still rules. Over the past 2500 years, large areas of forest have been felled and soil has eroded, leaving the sun-scorched land we see today.

One of the best-known Greek myths tells how Icarus used wax wings to try to escape captivity at the hands of King Minos of Crete, but he flew too close to the sun and fell to the sea when the wax melted. If he had been more cautious and managed to fly the length and breadth of the country, he would have seen at once how Greece's landscape encouraged the rivalries of its clans, shut off from one another by steep contours and natural barriers. He would have seen a series of long mountainous peninsulas fringed by narrow coastal plains. And he would have seen how the Indo-Europeans entered Greece from the north, across the great plains and steppes of Thrace and Macedonia.

The highest and most celebrated of the Greek mountains is Olympus (9570 feet). Its snow-covered peak was believed in ancient times to be the seat of the gods. Almost equally renowned is Mount Parnassus (8060 feet) whose summit rises above Delphi. Parnassus, part of the Pindos chain that stretches from the Yugoslavian border to the Gulf of Corinth, was the home of the Muses, and sacred both to Apollo and Dionysus, god of wine. It is now better-known as a skiing resort.

At different levels of the mountains, you will find different types of vegetation: starting with the olive at sea level, above that the oak, then scrub, juniper and pine. There is variation within the country too. In the Peloponnese, for instance, you find forests of black pine, while the harsher climate of the north favours such trees as the chestnut, giving the landscape a more Alpine feel. Greek mountainsides are often strikingly bare. This is due as much to human as natural causes. Forests have been cut down to give shepherds new pastures and farmers new land.

The mountains have always been an obstacle to the economic development of Greece, and indeed they still are. But they have also allowed the Greeks to maintain their traditional identity. During the four centuries of Ottoman occupation, many of the more independent-minded Greeks preferred to live in the mountainous areas, outside effective Turkish control, while the Turks exploited the more fertile areas of the plains.

The poor soils of the mountains encouraged the Greeks to turn to the sea for their livelihood – as well as to emigration. The mountains have also played a significant role in the country's religious history, with imposing monasteries perched on the rocky pinnacles of Meteora, on Mount Athos, and at Aghia Lavra in the Peloponnese, where the Greek War of Independence against the Turks was launched in 1821.

In the 20th century, Greece has struggled hard to

Previous page:
The curly-haired youth, the basket overflowing with grapes, the wine and the crusty bread ... all the images of a classical plenitude. In rural Greece, the world of antiquity never seems far away.

Harvest-time on the road to Andritsena. A peasant woman and her children return home after a day in the fields.

Greek fishermen haul in their nets. Thanks to overfishing and pollution, fishing has become less viable as a way of life in the past 30 years, although the price of fish has gone up dramatically.

catch up with the rest of Europe, turning its back on much of the past. There has been massive migration from the country to the cities, which have expanded chaotically to cope with their swollen populations. But, apart from a few pockets of development, the mountains remain the crucible of what the modern Greek poet Yannis Ritsos has called *romiosini* – roughly, 'Greekness', the nation's essential spirit.

To appreciate this, you have only to visit Epirus in north-western Greece. Here the climate is harsh, with heavy snowfalls in winter, and the landscape of thickly wooded gorges traversed by gurgling torrents is scarcely recognisable as Mediterranean. The architecture reflects this, too. The houses are tall, and the rooms have fireplaces with sleeping platforms on either side for the cold winter nights.

Ioannina, the main city of Epirus, has kept its character remarkably well. Built on the shore of a lake which it shares with some lovely Byzantine monasteries, the town is still rich in memories of Ali Pasha of Tepeleni, who ruled Ioannina and a wide area around from 1788 to 1822. In those days the town was not only the richest in Epirus and Albania, but one of the most influential and civilised centres in south-eastern Europe. (Ali Pasha, an Albanian by birth,

No wedding or saint's day feast is complete without music. Three of the most popular instruments in Greek folk music are shown here: accordion, fiddle and clarinet. Musicians will happily play right through the night, kept going by the wine, dancing, and offerings of money.

became too ambitious for his Turkish overlords in Constantinople – Istanbul – and they eventually sent troops to capture and execute him, which they managed to do only after a 15-month siege.)

In the oriental quarter of the town you can still see the old houses of Ali Pasha's time with their wooden balconies shaded by plane trees, as well as a charming little museum of folk art.

The whole of Epirus is fascinating. Some 12 miles north of Ioannina, in the area known as the Zagoria, lie a few dozen villages scattered through the mountains – now largely abandoned, although they bear witness to a prosperous past. Under the Ottomans, they grew wealthy through trade with Constantinople and through

the prosperity of those locals employed in the service of the Sultan. The region even had a degree of independence, despite the Ottoman yoke, and the villagers built themselves superb stone houses. Perfectly adapted to the difficult climate, the houses are built on three floors: the top for the summer; the first floor, with huge fireplaces, for winter; the ground floor for cellars, presses and storage. There is little chance of development here, so these villages are likely to remain as they are – images of a bygone age.

Happy Easter!

The Greeks are natural extroverts, who dramatise everything and experience life in vivid technicolour. You notice this everywhere, from the noisy arguments on street corners to the lurid 'home news' items in the press: life is tragedy or farce, with no holds barred and no grey areas in between. The attitude spreads to religious life, too. For many Greeks, the death and resurrection of Christ is an event as real as if it had happened the other day. Easter is the greatest festival in the church calendar – more important than Christmas.

Throughout Holy Week, the churches are full and the butchers' shops empty, as the faithful abstain from meat. On Good Friday, a public holiday, the fasting becomes more severe, with no animal products eaten at all (and that includes milk, butter, cheese and eggs). In the evening large candle-lit processions wind slowly through the streets of central Athens. Similar 'funeral' processions take place in every parish in Greece. For the death of Christ is an occasion for national mourning. On Holy Saturday, as the midnight hour approaches, crowds gather in town and village squares to wait in silence, with unlit candles, for the words of triumph to be spoken by the priest. As the clocks strike twelve, a cry goes up: *Christos anesti!* – 'Christ is risen!' *Alithos anesti!*, comes the crowd's reply. 'He is risen indeed!' Inside the church first one candle is lit, then another; then, as the flame passes quickly from person to person and out through the church doors to the crowd waiting expectantly outside, fireworks are set off, and in the streets and people's houses the greeting is exchanged a thousand times: *Christos anesti! Alithos anesti!*

The next morning, Easter Day, spring is in the air... and so is the smell of roast meat. Most families have a lamb on the spit which they cook slowly over a charcoal fire, often with *kokoretsi* (a long kidney and liver sausage in a gut skin). Family and friends crack hardboiled eggs, dyed red, together to see whose egg is strongest, the winner eating the loser's egg.

The informality and easy-going atmosphere of Greek religious ceremonies may come as a surprise to the foreigner, with members of the congregation coming and going throughout the service, greeting one another and chatting in church. This contrasts strangely with the sumptuous robes of the priests, the formality of the liturgy, and the solemn beauty of the icons that adorn the churches. This was true of Byzantine Greece too, where ordinary people were even closer to the earth than they are today, and the life of the clergy at least as rich in pomp and ostentation.

Every summer a festival is held at Epidaurus in the Peloponnese, a beautifully preserved theatre dating from the 4th century BC. Here the chorus rehearses in the circular playing area known as the orchestra. The 14,000-seat theatre has perfect acoustics: a whisper can be heard even in the furthest seats.

An Easter dance in the traditional foustanella *(skirts) and embroidered waistcoats at the village of Arachova, near Delphi. Dancing is a lively and important part of Greek social life. In this dance, baby goats are included as somewhat unwilling partners.*

A priest, known as papas, in his everyday black robes. Although marked out from the rest of the community by their clothes, long hair and flowing beards, priests lead otherwise ordinary lives. They are allowed to marry and have children; they cultivate their land, and can often be seen in village cafés drinking and chatting with their parishioners.

Preparations for Easter, the biggest church festival of the year, include baking koulourakia, sweet pastry plaits that often incorporate brightly dyed eggs.

After the fall of Constantinople in 1453, the Church had to concentrate all its energy on holding its ground under Turkish occupation. The Ottoman Sultans, keen to increase their grip on their possessions, exploited this. They confirmed the church patriarchs in their offices but also gave them a political function, with responsibility for maintaining the law. The clergy were trapped. They had no choice but to sacrifice their authority or to accept.

Yet, in spite of everything, the Orthodox faith was deeply rooted in the hearts of the Greek people, and was never seriously threatened. Throughout the Turkish occupation, the priests remained close to the people. They worked in the villages where they were born, educating the village children, and they played a major part in the revolution that led to the liberation of Greece. Indeed, the flag of independence was first flown by Archbishop Germanos at the monastery of Aghia Lavra in the Peloponnese.

The Church is still powerful, despite recent reforms which have introduced, for example, civil marriage and made divorce easier. The greatest threat to its influence is in the cities, where young people increasingly share the secularism of the rest of the Western World.

The Evil Eye

Alongside their religion, the Greeks continue to hold more ancient beliefs which 1600 years of Christianity have failed to wipe out. These may be the remains of an older, pagan religion, or simply traditional folklore. An intriguing example is the Evil Eye, or *kako mati*. This is a curse or evil spell which can affect people, animals, plants, or even objects, and is said to cause sickness, headaches, or tiredness in humans. People with the Evil Eye may be nasty types who wish ill on others, or they

may simply bring bad luck unintentionally. There is a story of a shepherd who noticed that his sheep were dying and suspected that he might have the *kako mati*. In order to test which eye was responsible, he closed one and looked at his sheep. Nothing happened. He then tried the other eye, and a sheep promptly died: at which point he is said to have torn out the offending eye and so saved his flock.

The Eye is often associated with envy. It singles out for attack anyone who possesses anything beautiful or fine: parents of new-born infants, children, couples engaged to be married, or the owner of a handsome animal. It is for this reason that expressions of admiration are regarded as particularly dangerous. To protect yourself from the Evil Eye you can spit, or make the sound of spitting – 'Ftu!' – or wear a little blue bead of glass with a black and white 'eye' set into it.

Such customs and beliefs are deeply rooted in the Greek character and still play a part in daily life. Take the following case of a young man with a headache. He has tried aspirins, but it won't go away; nor does the doctor have any explanation. So he goes to see a wise woman, who pours a few drops of holy oil into a cup of water. When an eye begins to form she knows the cause. '*Kako mati,*' she exclaims – someone, possibly an unlucky rival for a girl, has put the Evil Eye on him. The wise woman may then prescribe one of several remedies: she may say prayers or secret spells, then rub his head with a mixture of water and oil, or with salt. She will rarely take money for her pains.

Customs dating back to antiquity have been particularly well preserved in the north-eastern regions of Thrace and Macedonia. There, every year in May, at the feasts of St Helen and St Constantine, they hold the spectacular festival of the *anastenaria*. After a procession behind the icons of the saints, the villagers begin to dance. As the music becomes louder and faster,

The owl was the symbol of Athena, goddess of wisdom and patron of the city of Athens. Her helmeted head appeared on one side of ancient Athenian coins, the owl on the other.

Blue glass beads for protection against the Evil Eye. Despite a strong Christian tradition, belief in this curse remains widespread.

The miroloia *or funeral dirges are a way of celebrating the virtues of the dead person, and of expressing grief. They are rarely sung now, except in the remote villages of Epirus, Crete and Mani.*

Mount Athos in springtime. This rocky peninsula, known in Greek as Aghion Oros (Holy Mountain), is the domain of the Orthodox Church and dedicated entirely to the monastic life ... to the extent that no woman or even female animal is allowed to set foot there. It is a piece of the Byzantine world practically untouched by modern times.

some of the dancers, the *anastenarides,* go into a trance. When the trance reaches its height, they pick up the icons and dance, bare-footed, over a bed of hot coals, without coming to any harm. A flower-decked bull is sacrificed, meat is roasted, gallons of wine are drunk (though not by the fire dancers who tend to avoid alcohol), and the feasting goes on far into the night.

The origins of this custom are said to date back to the mid-13th century, when there was a disastrous fire in the church of St Constantine in the Thracian village of Kosti – now, in fact, part of Bulgaria. The church icons were heard groaning from the flames, and some of the villagers rushed in to rescue them. Miraculously, they were unharmed. In commemoration, their descendants repeat the miracle every year.

Karaghiozis the trickster

Despite the rapid advance of television into the sitting-rooms and bars of the nation, the traditional Greek shadow theatre survives. Under the glare of a 500-watt light bulb, with a scratchy record of clarinet music for accompaniment, it presents the life and works of Karaghiozis, a cunning peasant hero whose elaborate schemes constantly backfire.

Because of his large family and his preference for dubious ruses over regular work, Karaghiozis is always short of money. He stands about 10 inches high, a short, sturdy fellow with a tremendous nose and one unnaturally long arm which lashes out from time to time to clip his bumptious children on the ear. He is the

Straw is tied into bales after the harvest near Olympia. For thousands of years, Greek agriculture has been founded on the triad of wheat, olives and vines.

The design of this traditional wooden plough has not changed since the time of the rustic poet Hesiod (8th century BC).

The traditional threshing-floor (aloni), where grain is separated from the chaff. These can still be seen in many parts of rural Greece.

The women of Greece are the backbone of agricultural life, working every bit as hard as the men. If a woman's husband dies, she is expected to wear black for up to three years. After that she can wear lighter colours, but there must still be some black showing.

classic 'little man' with a wisecrack for every occasion, who somehow always ends up at the bottom of the heap.

Most of the stories are set in the time of the Turkish occupation. Apart from Karaghiozis himself, there are several other stock characters: Barba Yorgos (Uncle George), a shepherd from the mountains who wears the traditional *foustanella* or kilt; Velighekas, an Albanian, much disliked by Karaghiozis; Nionios, who comes from the island of Zakynthos; Stavrakas, a bully-boy from Piraeus; Morphonios, the pretentious Mr Know-All of the village, complete with outsize head; a benevolent Turkish Vizier; and Hadjiavatis, the town-crier in boots and tasselled cap, who is the favourite butt of Karaghiozis's constant flow of jokes.

As with Punch and Judy, there is terrific energy in the performances. The characters express the revenge of the

common people against their masters – whether occupying Turks or ambitious middle class. Karaghiozis himself is an image of the eternal Greek: fighting his way up with a mixture of cunning and native wit, boastful, daring, and full of grand but utterly impractical schemes.

Depending on the storyteller's style, the adventures are a bizarre mixture of ancient and modern history, with contemporary politicians, ladies from the Sultan's harem, and the proud, haughty figure of Alexander the Great all playing a part alongside each other. As in Italian *commedia dell'arte*, the plots are more or less standard, but the storyteller makes his own variations. The scenery too is standard: Karaghiozis's humble home, the Viziers's palace, the street outside the mosque. The silhouettes of the buildings are wedged up against the white screen. The puppets, made of brightly coloured gelatine, are held on rods and jointed at the hips, knees and shoulders, giving them great agility; their arms and legs are moved by sticks.

Music of the back streets

Everyone knows the sound of Greek music: the throbbing electric bass and the metallic, heavily accented pecking of the *bouzouki* that pours from jukeboxes and loudspeakers all over the country. For this is the music of Zorba's dance. Yet its apparent

'Blessed tree, invincible and immortal, food of our life, protected by Athena of the emerald eyes.' So wrote Sophocles, one of the three great playwrights of Classical Athens, in praise of the olive.

Practically everyone in Greece owns a few olive trees. After harvesting, the olives are taken to a communal press and crushed to make the oil which is the basis of Greek cooking. The best oil is sweet and mildly flavoured, with zero acidity on first pressing. Oils with higher acidity are refined to remove the harsh taste.

Traditionally, olives are harvested by knocking them off the trees with poles, then gathering them from the ground.

uniformity hides a remarkably rich and varied folk tradition. Modern popular music, an idiom used by many of Greece's serious composers, is a development of one strand of that tradition: *rebétika* or the songs of the *rebétes*. The *rebétes* were rough types: poor, semi-criminal bar-flies and drunks, the kind of people who carried knives beneath their jackets and were ready to use them.

They lived in the backstreets of ports, finding consolation for their outlaw existence in wine, women, music and hashish. Their songs are generally dark and defiant, though often with a humorous streak. They tell of bad luck in love, for example, of exile, death and imprisonment.

Rebétika reached its purest form in the 1920s and 1930s, when it was dominated by refugees from Asia Minor. They had come over – one and a half million of them – in an exchange of populations following a disastrous invasion of Turkey by Greece in 1919-22. They settled in the suburbs of Athens, Thessaloniki, Piraeus, and in towns and villages all over Greece, bringing with them their own special culture. To the music of Greece they brought the *outi* or Arabian lute, and the *santouri*, a kind of zither played like a xylophone, with a haunting, echoing sound.

The *rebétes* were usually self-taught musicians who accompanied themselves on the *bouzouki* or on its miniature cousin, the *baglamas*. Although a large number of recordings were made in the 1930s, *rebétika* was spurned by the more respectable Greeks until at least the 1950s. Since then, however, its popularity has grown immensely. Composers of international renown, such as Manos Hadjidakis (who wrote the music for the film *Never on Sunday*) and Mikis Theodorakis (who wrote the music for *Zorba the Greek*), as well as many of Greece's most popular singers, have acknowledged their debt to this bitter-sweet music of the dispossessed.

A small farm near Agrinion, in Akarnania, with its crop of tobacco plants. Greek tobacco is aromatic, like that of Turkey and Egypt, and is one of the country's minor agricultural exports.

The inheritors of the great *rebétika* tradition can be heard today in the *bouzouki tavernas* and clubs of suburban Athens and Thessaloniki. Greeks generally go to the *bouzoukia* on Saturday or Sunday evening. There is an important unwritten social code on these occasions, which you break at your peril. To interrupt or trespass on a solo dance, for instance, is a grave insult to the dancer.

Favourite dances are the *hasapiko* (butcher's dance), a celebration of companionship, with two or more men in line holding each other across the shoulders; the *zeibékiko*, a solo performance of deep and concentrated emotion, sometimes called the Dance of the Eagle; and the *tsiftetéli*, a lascivious, shimmying display, reminiscent of the belly-dance, which is openly erotic.

In the *zeibékiko*, a man will get up, throw a handful of

drachmas to the musicians, and take the floor. A friend goes down on one knee beside him and begins to clap a rhythm in time to the music. Fixing his attention on an invisible point at the centre of the floor, he starts to circle slowly, arms stretched out to the sides, his eyes cast down in the intensity of his concentration. In sudden bursts of energy he will swoop to the floor, spin, leap and strike his feet with his hands. The man may be young or old – it does not matter. What matters is that the right mood is on him, the *kefi* as the Greeks call it, a state of inspiration.

The Greeks still enjoy the famous practice of hurling plates to the floor in a rush of high spirits. With a grand gesture, a man who is feeling rich will push forward a pile of plates brought over by the waiter. The smashing interrupts neither dancers nor musicians. When the last plate lies shattered on the floor, the youngest waiter in the house, the *mikros,* sweeps up the mess while the dance continues around him.

Men and women

It is a day of celebration, for a baby boy is being christened. His *nonos* or godfather holds him proudly in his arms, wrapped in a shawl. At a given moment he removes the shawl and hands the naked child to the priest who plunges him into water three times, then anoints him with oil on the hands, feet, nostrils and ears. The infant, objecting loudly to these indignities, is bundled into a towel, and then dried and dressed in new christening clothes.

Gas rings have replaced the traditional wood-stove in the Greek home. Coffee is still made in the old way, though: a spoonful each of coffee and sugar per cup, stirred into cold water in a briki *or coffee-pot, and removed from the flame the moment it boils.*

To understand the modern Greek mentality, you need to know certain key words. One of these is *philotimo,* a word meaning both 'honour' and 'masculine pride', with a strong dose of 'what will the neighbours think?' *Philotimo* (literally, 'love of honour') drives the Greek male throughout his life. There is no room for self-doubt or self-deprecation. You only have to see an old man, one of those hardy, wizened, but immensely dignified characters bred by the mountains of Greece, to understand how strong this ideal is.

Related to *philotimo* are *andreia* (manly courage) and *levendia* (youthful zest, of body and mind). Physical strength, a noble spirit and unquestioning generosity: these are the manly qualities above all others. Relations between the sexes remain largely traditional, with the men lording it over the women. The pattern is changing, though – slowly in the villages, more quickly in the cities. Male children still tend to be coddled and spoiled. They are rarely scolded. Once the boy comes of age, he will be expected to play his part in keeping up the family's honour and good reputation.

A recent change in the law has allowed civil marriages and abolished the legal obligation to provide a dowry (*prika*). It is unlikely, though, that this ancient custom, which goes back at least 2000 years, will disappear entirely, at least in the near future. Dowries tend to be frowned on by the sophisticated, yet they can still reach fabulous sums when there is a wedding in a rich family. Shipowners have been known to give an oil-tanker away with their daughters. The dowry may not be necessary according to the law, but fathers continue to take pleasure in making a handsome gift to their daughters, commonly a flat or a house.

Feminists have attacked dowries as turning a woman into a piece of merchandise to be haggled over. It has to be said, though, that a flat in the wedding trousseau gives the young couple a healthy economic start, especially in Athens where the price of property – either bought or rented – is extremely high. The dowry, which by law remains the woman's property, also provides security for her. Whatever difficulties she may have in her married life, at least she will not be totally at the mercy of her husband when it comes to finances.

Some marriages are still arranged, although the practice is dying out. But even where a marriage is not formally arranged, an effort is usually made to find a more or less equal economic match. Greek society is very conservative, and encouraged to remain so by the Church. Recent years have seen difficult and sometimes violent conflicts between the generations, with parents

Weaving is one of the popular arts that has revived through tourism. Hand-woven cotton or wool cloth, with geometrical patterns or stylised embroidered designs, is deservedly popular.

who insist on the strict sexual codes of the past arguing bitterly with children who have absorbed the more free and easy ways of modern times. There are still girls who will not go out without a chaperone, and brothers who are literally prepared to kill anyone who dishonours their sister. But they are slowly becoming museum pieces, harder and harder to find.

Much has been said about Greece's relations with the past, and its struggles to break free from old ways of thinking. While this has meant new freedom for the young, improved health and communications, a general rise in the standard of living and the growing emancipation of women, it has also meant the disappearance of many colourful and unique folk-customs. One of the most unusual can be found in the Macedonian village of Monokklissia, north of Thessaloniki, where on January 8 each year men and women reverse their traditional roles: the men stay indoors to look after the children and do the domestic chores, while the women go out to the cafés, smoke, drink, play cards and talk politics. This extraordinary custom (all the more surprising in Greece's patriarchal society) was brought here by refugees from eastern Thrace in 1922.

A language resurrected

Tradition is also a matter of language. It is quite likely that Odysseus enjoyed eating roast lamb just as heartily as Greeks today, but what is certain is that he spoke the same language. The history of Greek began more than 2000 years before Christ, when the Hellenic group of languages first became detached from the Indo-European family. The earliest written Greek dates back to around 1500 BC, on clay tablets found at Mycenae and Pylos on the Peloponnese and Knossos on Crete. Although a different script, known as Linear B, was then used, its decipherment in 1952 by Michael Ventris and John Chadwick proved that the words represented were Greek. Today's language derives directly from the culturally and politically dominant Attic dialect of Athens of the 5th century BC.

The debate about right and wrong ways of speaking Greek goes back at least as far as Byzantium, where the ancient form of the language continued to be used for most writing, while the spoken language changed and developed. Many centuries later, at the end of the War of Independence, an uneasy compromise between the ancient, written language and the form of Greek spoken at the time was adopted as the official language of Greece, to the surprise and disappointment of the more liberal-minded supporters of the Hellenic cause.

This hybrid Greek proved to be impractical, however, and the other, everyday language of home and market-place, *demotiki*, eventually won the day. In 1917,

There is no single type of Greek looks, although the majority are dark, with deeply-sculpted faces.

In the market, sheep's wool is sold by weight, the price varying according to the softness and quality of the fibres. Sheep are also kept for their milk, which makes excellent cheese (feta and kasseri) as well as yoghurt.

The traditional Greek taverna is an informal place where you go into the kitchen to choose your food. Very often, as here, you eat and drink outside under a primitive roof of matting.

The kafeneion or café is still a strictly male preserve in most parts of the country. A man goes there to play cards, read the paper, and discuss politics over a cup of coffee or a glass or two of ouzo.

French, including such impeccably Greek-sounding words as *encyclopaedia* (which the French concocted out of three separate ancient Greek words); and, more recently, from English.

If you were sitting in a restaurant, and you asked the waiter for some *moussaka,* a steak with chips and salad, and a bottle of beer, you would say, 'Garson! Ena moussaka, ena bifteki me patates tiganites ke salata, ke mia bira.' The only words of pure Greek you would have used are *ena* and *mia* (one), *me* (with), *tiganites* (fried) and *ke* (and). *Garson* and *bifteki* come from French, *moussaka* from Turkish, and *patates, salata* and *bira* from Italian. The waiter will bring these things without batting an eyelid, but one wonders what Odysseus would have made of it all.

Flavours of the Greek countryside

Greece is not exactly renowned for its haute cuisine. The food can be very good, though, offering wholesome country dishes full of natural flavour that more sophisticated cooking tends to disguise. The vegetables, for instance, are usually grown without too many chemical fertilisers, harvested when fully ripe, and served fresh. Grilled fish and meat, too, can be delicious. It all depends where you eat. There is a big difference between home and restaurant cooking. A homemade dish of *moussaka* or *pastitsio* can be much less oily than its equivalent from a restaurant. The chances are that you will eat it more or less straight from the oven too, rather than lukewarm several hours later.

Meat is often rather tough – which explains why

Life is always lived as much outdoors as indoors, even in the relatively harsher climate of Macedonia – hence the tables and chairs set in the street. Inside, however, these houses also have carpets and thick woollen wall hangings and curtains, to keep out the icy blasts of the vorias *wind that chills the region in winter.*

A narrow village street in Epirus. Houses in the northern provinces could scarcely be more different from the dazzling white cubes of the Cyclades. Both winter and summer are harsh here. The sloping roofs with wide eaves provide shelter from the rain and snow, as well as shade from the sun.

against the powerful opposition of royalists, the Church and the parties of the Right, the Prime Minister Eleutherios Venizelos brought in *demotiki* as the language of education. The military junta who ruled Greece from 1967 to 1974 made a last attempt to re-instate the archaic language, *katharevousa,* by making it compulsory in schools and government, but this was a highly unpopular measure that effectively proved the kiss of death. In 1976, a law was passed unanimously in the Greek Parliament recognising *demotiki* as the official language, and leaving *katharevousa* to the arcane world of the legal contract.

Greek has had to borrow from other languages: from Turkish, inevitably, as this was the language of the administration that ruled the country from 1460 to 1830; from Italian, particularly the dialect of Venice; from

mince is so popular. Beef and lamb tend to come roasted in rough-hewn pieces on a bed of potatoes, or braised with tomatoes (*kokkinisto*) and served with macaroni. Aubergines, tomatoes, peppers, courgettes and stuffed cabbage leaves (*dolmadakia*) are almost always excellent.

Desserts and sweets such as *baklavas* and *kataifi*, made with honey, cinnamon, pastry and nuts, show a strong Turkish and Arab influence. Less well-known, but exquisite when properly made, are *loukoumades* (light doughnuts with cinnamon and honey) and *amygdalota* (almond cakes flavoured with orange blossom water and cloves and dusted with icing sugar). Other typical delicacies are the *glyka tou koutaliou* – cherries or miniature oranges in syrup – from Chios, and the *loukoumi* (Turkish delight) of Syros.

Fish is excellent but expensive. Best of all is *barbouni* (red mullet), although decent-sized ones are becoming increasingly rare. Other popular fish are *kalamarakia* (baby squid), *maridha* (whitebait), *synagridha* (sea bream), *ktapodhi* (octopus) and *garidhes* (prawns). Fish is always served with lemon, and when grilled on charcoal it is also likely to be flavoured with herbs.

The selection of cheeses is narrow. *Feta,* the best known, is often eaten with olive oil and oregano, or added to a *horiatiki salata* – tomatoes, onions, peppers, olives and cucumber. *Kasseri* and *kefalotiri* are harder, drier cheeses with a sharp taste reminiscent of Italian parmesan. Some good local cheeses can be found too.

Greek wine has improved dramatically in the past ten years, and it is now quite easy to get reasonable table wines either in shops or restaurants. *Retsina,* a white wine flavoured with pine resin, continues to divide people into passionate devotees and those who can hardly bear to look at it. Few tend to like it first time – though a recommended way to approach it is ice-cold,

with grilled fish, preferably in good company, on a hot summer's evening by the sea.

Traditional hospitality has suffered, inevitably, from the sheer numbers of tourists – Greece's population is doubled by incoming foreigners each summer. The old welcome, which so delighted travellers even 20 years ago, has been replaced in too many cases by commercial cynicism.

Occupation: shipowner

Greece may be the cradle of democracy, but it is one of the youngest states in Europe. And its struggle to overcome its economic disadvantages has been hard.

The two strongest sectors of the economy are tourism and shipping. The Greek merchant fleet is the largest in the world – if you take into account the owners whose vessels fly foreign 'flags of convenience'. In 1990, of a total world shipping capacity of 636 million tons, Greeks owned just over one-eighth. They also own close to half the tonnage of the European Community.

The biggest Greek shipping companies tend to have their head offices in London or New York, where the world's chartering is done. Crews, however, are generally recruited in Greece, with preference given to men from the owner's home island. Despite their often flamboyant international lifestyles, the owners like to keep strong links with their communities in Greece, returning every summer for their holidays.

The global primacy of Greek shipping is no historical coincidence, for the Aegean saw not only the birth of European civilisation, but also the earliest development of the arts of navigation. At first, sailing was a cautious matter of island-hopping and staying close to the coast. Later, more adventurous journeys were made, with

A barber's shop in suburban Athens sums up the bizarre mixture of architectural styles that you find in Greece. The two cement ladies with folded arms are in the neo-classical style favoured by Danish and German architects, which was brought to Athens in 1833 by the first king of modern Greece, Prince Otto of Bavaria.

regular trade between the Cyclades, Crete and Egypt, and then between Athens and its colonies in Sicily and Southern Italy. In the end, Greek mariners were sailing throughout the Mediterranean and into the Black Sea.

Even under the Ottoman Empire, despite heavy taxes on imports and exports by non-Muslims, Greeks (with Armenians and Jews) were the main traders. Later, the Greek merchant navy played an important part in both financing and equipping the fighters of the War of Independence of 1821.

The Greek shipping tradition can therefore be seen to have the deepest historical roots. It is bound up intimately with the nation's geography and with the character of the people. It is the biggest economic success story of modern Greece.

Leonidas and Co, Builders

One of the more intriguing survivals from Ancient Greece is the continued use of classical first names: Leonidas, Sophocles, Aphrodite, Aristotle, Miltiades... Walking along a village street, it is quite common to hear a high-pitched cry of 'Sophocles, lunch is ready!'

Feta cheese freshly cut from the block is for sale in this market in Athens. It is extensively used in Greek cooking, to accompany a salad, or in cheese or spinach pies, made with the thin leaves of pastry known as filo.

Much Greek food is stewed for long hours with oil, onions and tomatoes. Although the kitchen of a taverna may not look much, the owner will be happy to let his clients inspect the food before choosing what to eat.

or 'Antigone! Get your shoes on.' You turn, half-expecting a figure from ancient tragedy to appear, but instead you see a little child running to its mother.

If names have somehow survived the passage of 25 centuries, other elements of ancient Greek culture have not: the love of good architecture, for example. Most modern Greek houses are built fast and cheaply out of reinforced concrete. Mammoth white hotels glare out over the waters of previously unspoilt bays and, in the residential suburbs of towns, graceful 19th-century villas have often been demolished to make way for ugly but profitable blocks of flats. Fortunately, the authorities are beginning to reverse this trend; in particular, they are sponsoring a number of restoration programmes.

The countryside is emptying as the cities become more crowded, and even the bigger country towns are shrinking. The only rural areas to have maintained their old levels of population are the richer agricultural plains, where yields have been increased by irrigation, mechanisation, modern fertilisers and pest control.

Greece has not, until modern times, had a distinct urban tradition. Apart from the sudden influx of refugees from Asia Minor in the 1920s, most cities began to grow significantly only during the property boom of the 1960s. Athens, which has grown more consistently since the early 19th century, was once a charming neo-classical city. It is now a sea of concrete, jammed solid with traffic, and the most polluted capital in Europe.

In spite of this, Athens is still a remarkable place. It reflects in miniature the problems and charms of the country as a whole. In the suburbs, neighbours are usually friendly and conversations take place from house to house very much as they do in the villages on the islands.

Up to the time of independence, Athens was a relatively insignificant provincial town with a population of just a few thousand. It has grown into a sprawling capital of some 4 million inhabitants. There is a chronic shortage of green spaces. The roads are permanently full of cars – even after legislation to restrict traffic in the centre by allowing access only on alternate days on the basis of odd and even number-plates. Pollution is at dangerous levels.

Yet Athens has its magical places. Plaka, the old residential quarter beneath the Acropolis, has been closed off to traffic and its many lovely houses restored. Mount Lycabettus rises unspoiled right in the centre of the city, with wooded walks and spectacular views. Below it lies the elegant district of Kolonaki, where dinner is served at midnight and the cafés, cake shops and boutiques are as smart as any in Paris or Milan. Then there are the gardens of the Zappeion, the picturesque suburb of Kesariani, which was settled by refugees from Asia Minor in the 1920s; the quiet, leafy streets and squares of Kifissia; and the unrivalled splendours of the Acropolis and the Archaeological Museum. It is sobering to think – as one admires the human scale and harmonious balconied façades of the houses in Plaka – that most of Athens was like this just a few decades ago – and would have remained so but for the orgy of scruffy development that has seized the city since the war. Yet perhaps, one should also be grateful that so much of beauty has remained.

Piraeus has been the port for Athens since ancient times. It is the departure point for all the island ferries, as well as the recruiting centre for crews to man the largest merchant navy in the world.

Islands of Light

On Mykonos early in the morning, the main town, or Khora, is already dazzling in its whiteness. Its labyrinthine streets, which were laid out so as to confuse marauding pirates, are just coming to life. Peasants from the countryside trot into town on their donkeys with baskets of vegetables for sale. There was a time when they came to grind their corn in the windmills that stand above the town, but these have long been idle. The peasants go through the narrow streets and squares crying their wares: '*Melintzanes! Domates! Lemonia! Kolokithakia!*' ('Aubergines! Tomatoes! Lemons! Courgettes!'). The housewives come out to buy, scarcely noticing the tourists, the early bird out with his camera to capture a picturesque townscape, the late-night reveller lurching drowsily back to his hotel. They are used to each other by now, the tourists and the locals, having rubbed shoulders here continuously over the past 30 years. Mykonos became a tourist boom-island in the 1960s, invaded first by Athenians, then by the rest of the world. Some came to admire the ruins of the sacred island of Delos which sits half an hour away across a strait, but many come for the bare harsh beauty of Mykonos itself. Not only the landscape was bare, however. The island became

Girls from Skyros in their traditional costumes. Note the fine silks in rich colours, the velvet slippers embroidered with gold thread, the lace stockings and the long headscarves.

famous for its nudist beaches, neatly if informally divided into 'gay' and 'straight', and for its pioneering development of what has now become the standard Mediterranean holiday: sun, sea and sand by day, disco-dancing, drink and dalliance by night. Yet somehow the place retains its magic, and the local way of life continues much as it always has done.

After a long night's work, the bakers take the last loaves out of the ovens. People from the neighbourhood are already outside, waiting to buy bread and to bring in their baking tins filled with *moussaka, pastitsio* or stuffed tomatoes to cook slowly through the morning in the residual heat from the ovens. The doctor passes, soberly dressed in jacket and tie, a leather briefcase under his arm. He exchanges a decorous 'Good morning!' with them and continues on his way.

After the bakery, the second most important shop in town is the *pantopoleion* – literally the 'everything shop' or general store. Here you can buy paper, spices, perfume, soap, hardware and tools, newspapers, haberdashery and, of course, food. The shelves are crammed from floor to ceiling with a brightly coloured array of boxes and tins. Pots of honey keep carefree company with bottles of shampoo, candles and plastic flowers in this miniature supermarket, which somehow fits into a front room 14 feet square.

The scent of freshly ground coffee fills the air as you enter and the owner greets you with a tremendous smile, made bigger and friendlier by his impressive moustache. Shopping is still a highly social activity in Mykonos and you cannot do it properly without becoming involved in conversation.

There are two more institutions of island life: the retired government clerk, and the sailor home from overseas. Both are a kind of modern-day Ulysses. The first has an erudite air. He left home decades ago for a career in the Civil Service, working in government offices in Athens or Thessaloniki. He has books in his house and knows the history of the island. He is a source of practical know-how in dealing with officialdom – a useful and much respected skill.

The sailor has also been absent for years, but part of him has remained. There is always a mother, sister or wife who has news of him and keeps his photograph framed and polished on the sideboard. When he comes home, he builds a large house. He might open a restaurant or a small hotel with his savings. He has seen the world, or at least its ports: Tampa, Valparaiso, Yokohama, Southampton, Rotterdam, Calcutta. And in male company he will recount the nights he has spent in those places, seeking a sailor's pleasures to blot out the terrible nostalgia for home.

Some never return, leaving widows and mothers to a lifetime of mourning. At sunset, Urania, old and bent, dressed in widow's black, shuffles with tiny steps to the chapel. She holds the key, for she looks after the place. This morning she filled the vases with fresh flowers. Tonight she lights the oil lamp that hangs in front of the icon of St Nicholas, protector of ships. She crosses herself and kisses his holy image, and quietly shuts the door behind her.

Life in the Cyclades

Simplicity is the rule in the Cyclades. The houses are little more than white cubes, yet their construction perfectly matches materials and spaces with human needs. The sailors' homes make the most of little. The angles of door-frames and windows are softened and rounded by layer upon layer of whitewash. In one corner stands an earthenware water-pitcher, and opposite, a pot of basil. Tresses of onions hang drying over the door, and outside, in the bright sun, climbs a vine, which casts a deep shade. Everywhere is suffused by the dazzling light of the Aegean – the purest in the whole of Greece.

The house interiors are ageless and natural: a niche for the oil-jar, a space by the hearth for firewood, a little stone shelf for the lamp. The windows are tiny, to take the fury out of the light and to keep the house cool in the scorching summer, as well as to protect it from the icy winter winds. The fireplace is at waist height, making it easier to light. The house has just one room, 12 feet by 18, divided in two by a stone arch.

The roof is a flat terrace, whitewashed like everything else. It serves to collect rainwater, which is stored in a cistern under the house. Wood is scarce, so the ceiling is held up by just a few beams – the minimum necessary. The bed consists of a mattress laid either on a stone platform or on an internal balcony under which provisions are kept. Whether the building is a chapel, a house or a bakery, the structure is the same on islands all over the Cyclades.

Marina and Dimitri, an old couple who have lived

A young man from Skyros, dancing in the glazed blue cotton breeches and trohadhia *(open shoes). Traditions are particularly well-kept on this island.*

Old men of Skyros watch the world go by. More reserved than most Greeks, the Skyriots are outstanding craftsmen in wood, pottery and cloth. They let themselves go at their annual festival or *apokries* (carnival), just before Lent.

The white, flat-roofed houses of the Cyclades, with typically scorched dry hills above. This is Mykonos, many of whose finest houses and churches were built from the combined proceeds of piracy and fishing.

together for 70 years, are sitting out in the cool of the vine-covered pergola. It is some years now since Marina stopped baking her own bread, but she still goes to the well each morning, taking the narrow path between the lemon and pomegranate trees of their garden. The stone threshing-floor is covered in weeds now, but the wine-vats are still red from last year's vintage. Their children were here for that, and Dimitri trod the grapes with them. The wine is in a barrel in the storehouse.

The peasants age well here, for the island air is pure and the diet frugal. Marina makes cheese from the milk of their sheep, whose pen – tiny and white – is built into the rock. The bread oven curves out from the side of the house like the apse of a church. Just over the hill, the Aegean Sea stretches away in a vista of deep, almost purple blue. Above the vines stands the dovecote, a reminder of the Venetians who once ruled these islands: a little white tower of fretted stone. The lower part of the dovecote is used as a farm shed, and contains the primitive wooden plough that Dimitri used until just a few years ago.

The pigeons burble and coo up above. When the Venetians occupied this archipelago, from the 13th to the 18th century, they insisted on keeping birds – a practice that annoyed the peasants whose crops suffered heavily. Later, the sailing captains took homing pigeons on board ship to carry news home to their islands.

On these dry, rocky islands, the contours of the landscape are sketched out by the lines of dry-stone walls. 'May your fields go as far as your eyes can see and your house fit snugly round your shoulders.' That sums up the islanders' ideal – the way they have chosen to live, carving out the loveliest of homes for themselves in a place where the wind blows without pity, stone is plentiful and where wood is hard to find.

Few of the famous windmills of Mykonos are still in use. The triangular sails can be furled or unfurled according to the strength of the wind.

Wedding splendours and festive glories

In the islands, where tradition has a stronger hold than on the mainland, marriage is the crowning moment of a girl's life. It may be an arranged match, for these still exist; and there will almost certainly be a dowry, the fruit of many years' preparation.

At Astypalea, in the Dodecanese, weddings are held at the church built within the 13th-century *kastro* or Venetian citadel. Practically the whole village turns out for the occasion, crowding into the church courtyard in the late afternoon as the heat fades from the day. The interior of the church is brilliant with candles, their flames reflected in the gold and silver of its icons. The old women dressed in black, their heads covered with scarves, their gnarled hands folded in their laps, sit chatting in the wooden stalls. The bride now wears white, though once upon a time she would have worn the colourful local costume. As dusk falls, she arrives from her father's house. Leading the way are the musicians, dressed in dark suits and playing the bagpipes, the lute and the *bouzouki*. Behind them come the families of the bride and groom with the guests following them noisily into the church.

The three priests begin to chant the litany in fine resonant voices. It is hot and airless inside the church, with the press of bodies, the smoking incense and the candles. Children run in and out through the doors, while the adults distractedly follow the service, still chatting and greeting each other. The *koumbaros* or best man holds a pair of crowns made of orange blossom and linked by a white satin ribbon over the heads of the bride and groom, crossing them three times. The so-called 'dance of Isaiah' begins, the priest leading the couple around a special table laden with wreaths, flowers, rice and sweets in a walk that symbolises their journey through life in the steps of Christ. The wedding guests shower them with rice and flower-petals, while the priest and couple defend themselves as best they can from the high-spirited pelting.

The ceremony is over in less than an hour.

Afterwards, the family, followed by the rest of the village, make for the taverna, where the feasting and dancing continue through the night.

The other great occasion for a celebration in the village is the festival of the patron saint. This is known as a *panighiri*. It begins with a pilgrimage to the saint's chapel or church, which may be some distance from the village, in an isolated field or orchard. It ends as a great drunken picnic. The villagers use any means of transport they can find to reach the church, from donkeys and small, three-wheeler dump-trucks to air-conditioned coaches. If it is not too far, many will go on foot, dressed in their Sunday best, carrying flagons of wine on their shoulders and baskets filled with food in their arms. Most people make their own wine, and are keen for friends and neighbours to taste their produce. 'Tasting' however, is only half the story. The quantities consumed can be prodigious.

The priest – an imposing figure with a long beard and black robes – goes with the villagers, jovially chatting and joking. The church is opened, the candles and incense are lit. After the service, huge loaves of holy bread are brought out and shared among the congregation. Outside, under the blue sky, lambs are turning on spits and long trestle tables are loaded with wine, plates of tomatoes, bread and cheese. The villagers come out and then the festivities begin. The priest does the rounds of the families, stroking the children's heads. Everyone is happy. Under the olive trees the musicians strike up, and the singing and dancing get under way.

These scenes of country celebration, of festivities shared by the community, are part of an old pattern that was, until recently, common throughout Europe. A mixture of Christian and pagan, they marked the great turning-points of the agricultural year. In Greece, they suggest something more – a link with the religious rituals of antiquity.

The ancient Greeks believed in sacrifice as part of the religious ceremony. This led to a meal shared with the god, which allowed the participants to absorb his divine power. The cult of Dionysus, god of the vine and the rebirth of vegetation, was associated with orgiastic trances and hallucinations – a more extreme form of inebriation than you see today, although based on the same principle. Wine frees the spirit, uniting the community in mutual acceptance and goodwill. You will often hear people say, *'To krasi kani kalo'* ('Wine does you good') – a deeply held belief that goes back thousands of years. Yet excess of both food and drink is not habitual. These laughing, dancing and singing villagers lead extremely frugal lives for most of the rest of the year.

Another custom connected with saints is the name-day celebration. On St George's day, for instance, men by the name of George receive their friends and neighbours at home. Chairs are lined up along the walls of the front room and the visitors arrive, bringing cakes or brandy. *'Chronia polla!'* they wish him: 'Long life!' The priest comes too, and is the focus of conversation.

An old couple in Ios, the island where Homer is said to have died. Once controlled by the Venetians, Ios fell to Turkey in 1537 like many of the Cyclades.

A kitchen garden dug out of the poor volcanic soil on Patmos. St John, author of the apocalyptic Book of Revelation, dictated his great work on this island between AD 93 and 96. A monastery was built in his honour here in 1088.

It is a rather formal occasion, with no revelry or dancing. One man asks the priest for advice about a dispute he is having with a neighbour over the siting of a fence. Another opens a discussion about which musicians to call for the next *panighiri*. The others sit in silence, listening politely. As it grows dark outside, and between bouts of conversation, the sea can be heard down below, battering the rocky shore. Finally the party breaks up, and the visitors stumble home by torchlight, chattering more freely now, through the uneven streets.

When the boat comes in

Although the larger islands have airports with daily flights to Athens (and some to foreign cities), the only form of communication with the outside world for many continues to be by sea. All the islands are served by passenger ships – even the smallest and most sparsely populated. Some services are subsidised, and not all are direct to Piraeus: in many cases, passengers have to pick up a connecting ship at Syra.

Syra (or Syros) is the administrative capital of the Cyclades and, since the times of the Crusades, one of the few strongholds of Roman Catholicism in Greece. Its main town, Ermoupolis (named after Hermes, the god of commerce), was built by refugee merchants from the island of Chios who had fled there from Turkish massacres during the War of Independence. It is an elegant, solidly constructed 19th-century town, unlike any other island capital.

In the days of coal, it was the principal bunkering port of the Eastern Mediterranean. Ships on the Marseilles-Constantinople route would always put in here, and travellers to Greece would first set foot on her soil at Syra rather than Piraeus. Since 1893, however, when the Corinth Canal was opened, Syra has lost its primacy. The change from coal to oil-powered ships brought a further decline, although there are still thriving shipyards, cotton-mills and tanneries. The town of Ermoupolis itself has a faded, flaking charm, reminiscent of an old-fashioned Italian spa.

In this ancient seafaring land, it always comes as a surprise to see what poor sailors many Greeks are. The

Santorini is renowned for its tiny sweet tomatoes and for its wine. Vines are grown without supports, the tendrils coiling around themselves and the shoots extending along the ground. Peasants take their produce by donkey or mule to Fira, the capital, which is perched high above the sea.

Until the new port was built, the only way to Fira was by a steep mule track cut into the cliffs. Passengers arriving today can take a bus or taxi from the new harbour at Ormos Athinios. But the old methods are still used, with their hectic jostlings of the mules.

Known in Antiquity as Thera, the volcanic island of Santorini has had a long history of earthquakes. The last one was in 1956, when many of the houses built along the rim of the ancient crater slipped into the sea.

Aegean has frequent storms, particularly in winter, and the scenes on the quayside when the weather is rough are remarkable. *Epta Bofor!* (Force 7, Beaufort Scale). Passengers stand in the departure hall nervously drinking coffee and cramming themselves with biscuits, hoping to ward off sea-sickness with a full stomach. There is an air of final partings, of tragic farewells. Among them, smoking calmly, are the lorry and tricar drivers, the exporters of fish, fruit, *loukoumi* (Turkish delight) and vegetables. They are used to it all and have been through much worse than this.

Bad weather, though, remains a serious matter. In the worst winter storms, shipping timetables are disrupted, the post fails to arrive, journeys have to be postponed, and anyone with urgent business in Athens simply has to wait. The ships, too, are often overcrowded. One can well understand why Greeks habitually make the sign of the cross before they travel.

On a few islands, especially those with a roadstead but no deep-water port, the business of embarking and disembarking can be difficult. It was notoriously hard at the volcano-island of Santorini before the new harbour

was built. In bad weather the ships would sail round to enter the harbour – a huge flooded crater 18 miles around the rim – from the leeward side. The sea was covered in a layer of freshly-formed pumice; the sky was leaden; the island's weird and blasted volcanic rock black and sinister-looking.

The shore-boats would venture out to pick up passengers and be forced to hover at the side of the ship, using up their precious petrol, while they waited for the swell to die down. If the waves remained high, they would make for the shore again, to return an hour or two later. Sometimes, even then, the leap from the door in the ship's side to the frail, pitching shore-boats would seem too risky to the assembled passengers, until some brave soul – a priest perhaps – crossed himself and jumped into space ... to be caught by the sure-handed boatmen down below. His bags would follow.

Then, inspired by his example, the rest of the passengers would do the same, and the ship could finally sail on towards its next destination, leaving the tiny shore-boats to battle their way through the waves to the foot of the towering cliffs.

Much of the charm of Greece lies in its openness to the elements. This of course means storm as well as sun, and island Greeks retain a daily contact with nature which most city-dwellers have lost. The anxiety and beauty of travelling by sea, its slowness, its romance, its genuine dangers – even in the late 20th century – contribute much to the sense of continuity you feel in the islands. You see people today travelling very much as their grandparents did, experiencing the same sensations, living their lives at an older, gentler, possibly saner pace.

Every islander likes to have a garden or a piece of land, however small, to grow figs, lemons, oranges, grapes and vegetables. The land needs constant watering and care, though. Here a man carries home the trimmings from his fig-tree.

Coffee time in Patmos. The island's capital, with the fortified Monastery of St John, sits on a crag 150 yards above the sea.

Icons and pilgrimages

In almost any church in Greece you will see silver votive offerings hanging from lamps or icons. These are made to saints in thanks for cures and other favours: a successful operation, a son returned safe from a dangerous voyage, a prosperous year's fishing. The greatest votive act of all is the pilgrimage to the island of Tinos in the Cyclades. On August 15 each year, the festival of the Assumption of the Virgin, thousands of pilgrims gather in front of the miraculous icon of the Immaculate Conception in the church of the Panaghia Evanghelistria. For days beforehand the passenger ships have been bringing them in: invalids in wheelchairs, the halt, the lame, the sick, accompanied by their families carrying cardboard boxes, parcels and suitcases, baskets of food, water, blankets. The baggage would seem enough for a month's siege, though in fact it is merely provisions and bedding for just one or two days, the hotels being full. And the cures? Do they really happen? Reputedly, they do – and so it would appear from the fantastic number of silver offerings in the shapes of limbs and organs – feet, legs, eyes, hands – hanging from the icon to express gratitude to the Virgin Mary for her miraculous intervention.

Pilgrims are expected to travel the few hundred yards along the road from the quayside to the church on their knees. The crowds are enormous and, being Greek,

An islander sells koulouria, *sesame bread rings, on Tinos, where the discovery of a miracle-working icon of the Virgin Mary led to the annual pilgrimage on August 15. Tinos is the Greek equivalent of Lourdes.*

somewhat panicky. Everyone is afraid of not getting off the ship in time, of not finding a place to sleep, not managing to reach the church to kiss the icon and light a candle.

Carnival in Skyros

Despite the revolution in social attitudes in Greece over the past 20 years, despite membership of the European Community, satellite television, the tourist boom, jet travel and a host of other changes, old traditions die hard. The carnival in Skyros is a good example.

Skyros is one of the islands of the Northern Sporades, some 75 miles north-east of Athens. According to legend, Thetis hid her son Achilles in the king's palace here, disguised as a girl, to prevent him from going to his prophesied death in the Trojan war. The trick would have worked but for the wily Odysseus, who gave presents to the girls at court that included a beautifully-made sword, which Achilles betrayed himself by choosing.

Skyros has a long tradition of goat and sheep-herding that goes back at least to Classical times. Its folk traditions, both in music and in the arts of embroidery and wood-carving, are strong. The island has a particular significance for English visitors as the last resting-place of Rupert Brooke, who died of septicaemia near here on a hospital ship while on his way to Gallipoli in 1915. His grave lies in an olive grove near the island's southern tip. His poem 'The Soldier' is one of the most famous in the English language:

> If I should die, think only this of me:
> That there's some corner of a foreign field
> That is for ever England ...

Carnival in Skyros is a lively occasion, a time of wild revelry before Lent. The festival is known as *apokries*

Small-scale fishing is as important on Samos as on the other Greek islands. Unlike many of the other islands, however, Samos – which lies less than 1¹/2 miles off the Turkish coast – is well-wooded. It also produces a famous sweet white wine.

The rocky shore of Ithaca, isle of Odysseus, rises steeply behind a brightly painted fishing vessel. Since Odysseus's time the Ionian island group, to which Ithaca belongs, have had a number of overlords, including the Romans, the Venetians, the French and the British, before they were finally returned to the Greeks in the 19th century.

Dolphins gambolling round the boat are one of the delights of sea travel in Greece. Some wonderful frescoes depicting dolphins were found at Akrotiri on Santorini, dating from the 15th century BC.

The price of fish may have gone up in recent years, but the Greek fisherman's life remains hard – most of the profits going to the middle-men. Moreoever, the Greek seas, especially the Aegean, are notoriously treacherous: winds whip up suddenly from nowhere and the fishing boats barely have time to reach a safe anchorage where they can ride out the storm.

(the name means 'meat away', just as 'carnival' does in Latin). During *apokries* the streets of the main town come alive with strange devilish-looking figures moving to and fro amid the deafening sound of bells. Young men who have left the island to work in Athens come home for the last three hectic days of the festival. They put on the black goatskin cloak of the *geros* (old man) and a mask of kid-leather. They load themselves with belts of heavy copper bells weighing over 100 pounds and rove through the streets all day until they are exhausted.

It is all strikingly reminiscent of ancient fertility rites, celebrated at the start of spring to ward off evil influences and to ensure a good harvest. Or is it – as some think – a relic from the worship of an ancient shepherd god, now long forgotten? The island's economy has always depended on its flocks of sheep and goats, and shepherds are vitally important figures. The costume of the *geros* certainly suggests a shepherd, with its cloak and bells. And it has been noted that similar costumes are worn in other pastoral communities, not only in Greece (in Macedonia and Eastern Thrace, for example) but elsewhere in Europe and beyond.

The people of Skyros have their own version of the origin of their festival. An old shepherd and his wife were guarding their flock high in the mountains at the time of *apokries,* when a sudden violent fall of snow killed all their animals. The shepherd decided to make the best of the situation, skinned the flock, loaded the

geros to dress: the white woollen breeches, the *kapoto* (cloak), the mask, and most importantly the stout cord strung with bells. This has to stand up to hours of shaking and rattling, and must be securely tied. The trick is to go along the main street without being recognised, then slip into an alley to catch your breath or to call in on a neighbour for refreshment. The *geros* has two aims: to last out the day, which requires enormous physical endurance, and to produce a spectacular sound with his bells, both rhythmically and dynamically, through the movements of his body.

The harvest is brought home in Crete. This huge island, 165 miles long, was the home of the Minoan civilisation. Despite its mountainous terrain, it has become one of the major agricultural areas of Greece.

hides and bells onto his shoulders, and returned with his wife to the village. The villagers were so amazed by the grotesque sight of the old shepherd weighed down with so many goatskins and bells that they decided to repeat the spectacle every year at that time.

The costumes are made with immense care. When the time comes to put them on, the whole family helps the

The *geros* is usually accompanied by two other figures: the *korela*, a young man dressed in the traditional woman's costume of the island, but with the addition of a kid-leather mask and a shepherd's thick stockings and shoes. The *korela* dances around the *geros*, waving a handkerchief. There is also the comical figure of the *Frangos* or European (literally a 'Frank'), dressed in 17th-century European costume but also masked, with a large bell tied to his back and a sea-shell in his hand which he blows as he walks along.

After the day's wanderings, the carnival figures make for the Monastery of St George, patron saint of the island, and do homage to his icon. A great final ringing of bells brings the ceremony to an end, and the revellers go home to take off their costumes before coming out again for a night of dancing, music, food and wine.

On the morning after, the men walk slowly, dragging their feet with exhaustion. The grocer does not even get up to open his shop. Those who work in Athens must begin the long journey back to their 'exile'. The goat-skins are put away for another year, and Skyros returns to normal 20th-century life.

The summer heat on Crete has an almost African ferocity – which is not surprising since the island lies roughly as close to Africa and Asia as it does to mainland Europe. The character of the Cretans reflects this harsh climate: they are rugged, proud, fiercely resisting foreign overlords.

A Cretan shepherd in the traditional headdress of the island makes himself a bamboo flute. The largest flocks are to be found on the Omalos plateau, some 3000 feet up in the Lefka Ori or White Mountains.

Palm trees and eucalyptus grow readily in Crete, proving the mildness of its winters. Although it is a peaceful place now, much favoured by tourism, Crete was renowned for centuries for its fierce resistance to foreign invaders. The Turks took 25 years to complete their siege of Candia in the 17th century, and the airfield at Maleme witnessed one of the most ferocious battles of the Second World War.

Crete – island of fighters

One of Crete's special holidays celebrates – characteristically – an episode from its centuries-long struggle against foreign overlords, in this case the Turks who ruled the island from 1669 to 1898. Between November 7 and 9 each year, all work stops, and local and national dignitaries gather for commemorative ceremonies at the Arkhadi Monastery on the mountain slopes above the north-coast town of Rethimnon. Here, in November 1866, 40 Orthodox monks, 259 Cretan partisans and nearly 700 women, children and old people were besieged by an army of 16,000 Turks. In spite of the impossible odds against them, the defenders managed to hold out for two days. Finally, as the Turks were beginning to break through into the main part of the monastery, the abbott decided on drastic action. Surrender was out of the question, so he ordered one of the partisans to set a fuse to their supplies of gunpowder and ammunition. In the resulting blast – whose echoes were heard throughout Europe, triggering a wave of anti-Ottoman feeling across the continent – 829 people were killed, besieged and besiegers alike.

The Cretans have always been something of a race apart from the rest of the Greeks. They won their freedom from Turkey later than many parts of the country (the island only became an official part of Greece in 1913), and because of their central position in the eastern Mediterranean – as close, more or less, to Africa and Asia as to Europe – they have always been exposed to a greater variety of outside influences. They are obstinate and heroic fighters, who proved their metal not only against the Turks, but also against the Germans in the Second World War. They also have a reputation for lawlessness – blood feuds were common in mountain villages well into this century – and for being wily in their business dealings. They already had a well-established reputation in the lifetime of St Paul, who wrote: 'Even one of their own prophets has said, "Cretans are always liars, evil brutes, lazy gluttons" ' – the 'prophet' in question being Epimenides, a Cretan philosopher. On the other hand, they have a consistent record of producing men of genius: from the Cretan-born painter El Greco (properly, Domenikos Theotokópoulos) in the 16th century to the novelist Nikos Kazantzakis (author of *Zorba the Greek*) and the composer Mikis Theodorakis in the 20th century.

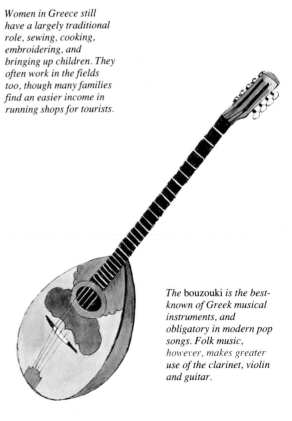

Women in Greece still have a largely traditional role, sewing, cooking, embroidering, and bringing up children. They often work in the fields too, though many families find an easier income in running shops for tourists.

The bouzouki *is the best-known of Greek musical instruments, and obligatory in modern pop songs. Folk music, however, makes greater use of the clarinet, violin and guitar.*

As befits people who have always lived by their wits, the Cretans have cheerfully embraced tourism in recent decades, allowing hotels and self-catering apartment blocks to engulf many of the small fishing ports of the north coast. But they have not let it destroy their island. Inland and on the south coast much remains as it has been for centuries: narrow coastal plains and rocky mountain slopes clothed in olive groves, vineyards and citrus orchards (Crete's other source of wealth); ancient villages sparkling white in the Mediterranean sun. Peasants driving donkeys vie with motorists and the drivers of trucks and buses for the use of narrow, twisting mountain roads. You still sometimes see old men sitting out in village squares wearing their traditional baggy black trousers (*wraka*) – indeed, some younger Cretans have also taken to wearing the *wraka*, as an emblem of their patriotism.

The spectacular, 11-mile Samaria Gorge in the White Mountains (Levka Ori) of the west has long since surrendered its untamed wildness to the demands of tourism, but many other mountain spots survive much as they were when local *klephti* (bandits) used them as bases for preying on the surrounding lowlands and harrying the hated Turks.

Nowhere is the continuing vitality of Crete's distinctive way of life more evident than in its folk culture. Cretans, like all Greeks, turn out in force for weddings and religious festivals, and as always music, singing and dancing are a key part of the proceedings. No celebration would be complete, for example, without the bandying to and fro of *mantinades*. These are uniquely Cretan: rhyming couplets, each line with 15 syllables, which local people have an extraordinary capacity for composing on the spot. Sometimes a kind

of rally will get going, with different people in a group making up ever more elaborate couplets to cap those that have gone before. *Mantinades* may be witty or sad, bawdy or uplifting, as the occasion demands. And they are not just for special holidays: sometimes people exchange them with friends in the street; men can be seen sitting in bars in the evenings whiling away the time as the couplets fly between them.

Mantinades are by definition impromptu compositions, but the Cretans also have a rich repertoire of traditional songs. Many of these celebrate the resistance heroes of old, among the most famous being the 'Song of Daskaloyiannis', which commemorates the deeds of the wealthy patriot Yannis Vlachos. He led a rebellion against the Turks in the 1770s and met a particularly gruesome end: the Turks eventually lured him into a trap and then publicly executed him by skinning him alive, in front of a large mirror. Another popular group of songs are the *rizitika tragoudia* (literally, 'songs from the roots') which originated among the villages of the White Mountains. These are often more domestic. Many celebrate the heroism of the old resistance heroes and themes such as the bonds of family, village solidarity and friendship, but others were composed to be sung around the table *(tavla)* in honour of a patron saint or baptism or the like. Among the most moving of the *rizitika* songs are those that used to be sung during wedding festivities as the family and friends of the groom made their way along the mountain roads to the village of the bride. Such processions are rare nowadays, but the songs they sang are still an essential ingredient of any traditional marriage.

Cretan music and dancing is equally distinctive. The music with its complex rhythms and endlessly repeated

Most bakeries now use electric ovens, although a few are still fuelled with wood. This gives the bread a unique flavour. Many bakeries continue the old tradition of letting people use the ovens for their own baking once the bread has been taken out.

Most Greek wines lack depth and subtlety, but the production of table wines has improved greatly in the past few years. Retsina, flavoured with pine resin, is the most distinctive, but it is very much an acquired taste.

Water is scarce in summer, and has to be imported to some islands in tankers. The system of collecting rainwater in cisterns, however, allows the islanders to indulge their passion for gardening and for decorating their front doors with potted plants.

Water melons are one of the best sources of refreshment in the hot summer months. The whole fruit is used: the seeds are dried and eaten, and the skins fed to animals.

The body of Spyridon, patron saint of Corfu, is carried around the town in one of several annual processions. Spyridon is famed for his protection both of individuals and of the community – from plagues, earthquakes and attacks by the Turks. His shrine is richly loaded with votive offerings from thankful believers.

melodies has a much more oriental feel to it than that of the rest of Greece. Inevitably, it has a rival among young Cretans in the modern pop and rock music that blares out from many of the bars and discos of the towns. Even so, people young and old remain loyal to their traditions. Many play the Cretan *lyra*, a three-stringed instrument played with a bow while held upright on the knee; the high-pitched drone of the *askomantoura*, a kind of twin-piped flute, sounds out from the cassette players of taxi dashboards. And as

essential to any traditional festival as the *rizitika* songs and *mantinades* are the various Cretan dances, above all the *pentozalis*, the mesmerising dance from eastern Crete. As with all the most famous Greek dances, the dancers form a row, holding on to one another around the shoulders. The music starts slow, then gradually quickens in pace as the steps become more complicated. One by one the dancers break from the row to perform a series of highly acrobatic manoeuvres which include snapping the heels together in mid-air, before rejoining their fellows and letting the next soloist take his turn.

Invaders

It is easy, when visiting Greece, particularly on a summer holiday, to forget the extraordinary wealth of its history. The Greeks had already known 2000 years of civilisation before the birth of Christ. First there were the impressive Bronze Age Helladic and Minoan cultures of the Cyclades and Crete, believed to have been dealt a mortal blow by the eruption of Thera (modern Santorini) probably around 1700 BC.

Then there were the Mycenaeans, whose exploits were chronicled in Homer's *Iliad* and *Odyssey*, and whose supremacy ended shortly after the Trojan War traditionally dated around 1200 BC. And eventually there were the city-states of Classical Greece, the greatest of which was Athens, whose heyday was in the 5th century BC. Greece became a province of the Roman empire in 147 BC, although the political and intellectual ideals of Rome had been largely formed according to Greek models. From the end of the Roman period (AD 330), the rule of Byzantium alternated with brief episodes of Hun, Slav and Arab control of some parts of the country, with pirates a more or less continuous threat. The Venetians, leading the Fourth Crusade of 1204, sacked Byzantium and distributed its empire among the French and Italian crusading lords, but they in turn were harassed and in many cases ousted from their possessions by the Ottoman Turks. Byzantium fell to them in 1453, Athens in 1458. Crete remained in Venetian hands until the Turks took Heraklion after a terrible 25-year siege in 1669.

The Turkish occupation, known in Greek as the *tourkokratia*, was the one that hurt most. It lasted for more than 400 years. Although Christianity was tolerated, the Greeks were a subject race whose social, economic and political growth was stunted. The democratic institutions which the ancient Greeks had invented, and which, in the wake of the Renaissance, other nations were slowly developing between 1450 and 1850, did not have a chance in Greece. It is no exaggeration to say that Greek society is still trying to recover from its long dark age of foreign occupation.

From the 15th to the 19th centuries the seas of Greece were a more or less constant battleground – involving pirates, Turks, Venetians, other west Europeans and the warriors of Greek independence. Underlying it all, though, was the confrontation between Christianity and Islam, the cross and the crescent, which was represented for much of that time by Venice and Istanbul.

The 350-year struggle between Venetians and Ottomans left highly visible marks on the Greek islands in the form of fortresses. Known locally as the *kastro* or *frourio,* these imposing stone citadels, built on natural eminences of rock, still stand today. Their steep-walled bastions dominate countless island capitals from Corfu to Crete. From the villages that clustered around them, the inhabitants would flee along alleys and tunnels to the safety of the fortress, leaving their houses to be pillaged by corsairs or soldiers. Many of these great castles are now falling into decay – succumbing to neglect after standing up to centuries of war.

The Ionian Islands never fell to the Turks, despite many fierce attacks and brief periods of occupation, and only passed from Venetian hands when the Republic of Venice itself was dissolved by Napoleon in 1796.

At the start of the 19th century, the island of Hydra, off the east coast of the Peloponnese, became a centre of Greek resistance to the Turks. The island's shipowning families were persuaded to place their fortunes and energies at the service of the struggle. They armed corsair fleets, such as those of Miaoulis whose harrying tactics against the Turks soon gave the insurgents control of the sea.

A few years later, on March 25, 1821, the standard of rebellion was raised at Aghia Lavra in the Peloponnese. It was a great moment, which to this day no Greek is allowed to forget. Every year the anniversary is celebrated with fanfares and parades, even in the smallest village. The mayor makes a speech, followed by the priest, commemorating the heroes who died for their country. Schoolchildren perform favourite scenes from the struggle, complete with costumes, make-up and oriental props.

The year after the events at Aghia Lavra, a young girl from Euboea, Manto Mavrogenous launched a series of successful attacks on the Turks from a base in Mykonos. She raised an army of young soldiers, inspired by her beauty and fiery leadership. They went into battle wearing white linen, with flowers behind their ears. Manto's defeat of the Turks was vengeance for her father's death, but she was avenging many other Greek deaths too.

Although the independent Greek state was officially recognised by the major European powers in 1830, only about half the territory of modern Greece was under its control at that time. The northern half of the mainland remained Turkish, as did the eastern half of the Aegean and Crete, with the Ionian Islands under a British Protectorate. Crete threw off the Turkish yoke after a

The komboloi, *originally a rosary, carries no religious meaning. It is carried and fingered by men as they sit in cafés; the de luxe version is laid out on the coffee tables of middle-class sitting rooms.*

Candles play an important part in the ritual of religious worship in Greece. They are lit and placed before icons to accompany a personal prayer, and on Good Friday they light the great funeral procession of Christ, the epitaphios, *that winds through the street of every parish in the country.*

successful rebellion in 1896, but was not officially united with Greece until after the First Balkan War of 1912. The same war also brought Greece Ioannina, Thessaloniki, Chios and Mytilini.

This century has seen other turmoil too. As well as the Balkan Wars of 1912-13, there have been the two World Wars, the ill-fated expedition to Anatolia in 1919-22, and the attempted takeover of the country by Communists in the Civil War of 1944-9. In 1947, while this last struggle was going on, Rhodes was ceded to Greece by Italy.

The most recent invaders are the tourists. Few parts of Greece have escaped their attention. Reinforced concrete hotels have sprouted like mushrooms, often without any respect for the beauty or natural grandeur of the spaces they occupy. Towns and landscapes have been transformed – rarely for the better. Pizzerias have pushed out the old tavernas where customers once went into the kitchens to choose their food. Plastic chairs have replaced the friendly old wooden ones with straw seats, which seemed to have been in Greece since time began. In many cafés and bars now, you can no longer have Greek coffee: only instant is served.

The tourist boom now shows signs of slackening, but in many places the damage has already been done: to the environment mainly, but also to the traditional skills, dignity, customs and attitudes of the people. Tourism has, of course, brought money, which is sorely needed in such a poor country; but much of it has been easy money, bringing with it the expectation of more easy money. At times it appears a corrupting influence for a people whose spirit has been shaped by the struggle to make a living from mountainous land and an unforgiving sea. There is a Greek proverb, much quoted by the shipping community when the market is down and times are lean: *i thalassa arosteni alla poté then petheni* – the sea becomes ill but never dies. The same thing might well be said about the Greeks themselves, and their country.

To appreciate both, visit Greece off-season, preferably in autumn, when the weather turns mild and the sea is still warm, and the tourists have all gone. Then the real Greece can be seen. The countryside comes alive again after the first rains, and the air is full of vivid autumn smells: pressed grapes, dried figs and *ouzo,* bonfires of olive and cypress twigs that give off a rich aromatic smoke. The men of the village turn hunters and stride out over the hills with their shotguns and dogs. Migrating birds fill the sky.

The village cafés, empty of tourists now, turn back into informal parliaments, where the problems of the world are thrashed out among games of cards, bottles of wine and clouds of cigarette smoke. The café is still a man's world, rarely entered by women unless to haul out their husbands for a telephone call or some urgent business. Despite the inevitable television flickering in one corner, the *kafeneion* retains its place as the hub of village life. In this raucous, witty assembly, in which nothing is sacred except the right to express your opinion as loudly and forcefully as you can, you can see the Greeks re-inventing philosophy and democracy before your eyes. As the rain lashes down outside you feel that this is still, in a curious way, the centre of the civilised world.

Petros the pelican, the most celebrated and photographed citizen of Mykonos. When he disappeared to the nearby island of Tinos, he was the subject of a lawsuit which succeeded in bringing him back. Since then another Petros has appeared in Tinos, enjoying the same success as his rival, although some suspect that they are the same bird cunningly turned commuter.

Italy

For centuries, Italy has been a place of pilgrimage for artists,
writers and travellers. No civilised gentleman's education was
complete without a trip to Florence, Rome and Naples. Today,
the tourists are numbered in millions. But the attraction of Italy
cannot be explained simply in terms of its art treasures,
unparalleled as they are, or its historic importance as the
birthplace of two civilisations – Roman and Renaissance. There is
something more: a liveliness in the Italian people themselves that
gives even the simplest transaction – ordering a cup of coffee or
asking the way in the street – a special zest and beauty.

In the Middle Ages most city bridges were inhabited. The Ponte Vecchio in Florence is one of the rare remaining examples; it is now mainly occupied by jewellers, who keep up a tradition for which the Florentines have been famous since the 15th century.

Florence, city of the Renaissance. The Ponte Vecchio is on the left, and on the right is the unmistakable profile of the Duomo (Cathedral). The dome was designed by the Renaissance sculptor, engineer and architect Filippo Brunelleschi.

Previous page:
Fountain of Neptune, Piazza della Signoria, Florence. It was here that Girolamo Savonarola, the religious and political reformer, was publicly burnt in 1498 – a reminder that life here has not always been sweetness and light.

Land of Renaissance Glories

Any traveller coming into Italy from the north has a feeling of entering a separate world. Before the age of motorised transport, the great bristling curve of the Alps, stretching from Nice to Trieste, posed a formidable barrier, shutting off Italy from the northern half of Europe. You can still sense it today if you make the trip by land: the points of entry to Italy are few, over high passes or through long tunnels; the journey is hard and long. Even when you view the Alps from a plane, the frozen ocean of jagged white peaks below has something daunting about it. And the flight – two hours from England – seems much too short for the gulf you have crossed between cultures: from the grey light of London or Birmingham to the dazzling brightness of Rome. History jumps too, as you make that sudden transition from concrete metropolis to Renaissance city – a time leap that is almost too much for one's mental clock to handle.

It would be better to arrive slowly, at the pace of, say, Hannibal's elephants. You would then discover Italy by stages, the way conquerors and artists have done for centuries, entering through Italy's transition zones. These can be quite a surprise if you have never come across them before: French place names and French-speaking inhabitants in the Val d'Aosta; and everything in German – road signs, food, costumes, greetings – in the Alto Adige. Then, having been gently introduced to Italy, you descend through the foothills to the Po plain – the *pianura padana* – with its network of motorways and railways connecting an array of gorgeous cities.

Those of Italy's conquerors who made the difficult Alpine crossing tended to assume that the worst was behind them and that it would all be straightforward from now on. They were usually proved wrong. In the winter of 1077 the German Emperor Henry IV had to wait humbly for three days outside the gates of the Castle of Canossa before Pope Gregory VII would revoke his excommunication. King Francis I of France found himself taken prisoner in Pavia in 1525 after an unexpected defeat in battle. These and others succumbed to the Italians' notorious 'elastic' defence: letting the invaders come, whoever they were – Carthaginians, Gauls, Byzantines, Normans, Arabs, Austrians – and often getting on with their lives while the conquerors worked off their fury, became corrupted and besotted by pleasure, or lost heart and went off to make trouble somewhere else. Even today's less hostile visitors go through a similar process. Italy has a way of sending them home changed, less sure of their ambitions, filled with the unsettling knowledge that the best things in life are simple, uncomplicated, and usually Italian. They often find the country hard to leave.

A natural paradise

Out of reach of the foggy Po plain and protected by the Alps from the icy north wind, the Italian lakes of Maggiore, Como and Garda have a special, temperate climate: neither too hot in summer nor too cold in winter. The temperature rarely drops much below 3° or 4°C (37° or 39°F); olive and lemon trees flourish. The 19th-century French writer Stendhal, who used to enter Italy through the lakes, said that he always had the feeling of passing from winter to spring as soon as he crossed the frontier.

It would be wrong, though, to assume that the weather in the rest of Italy is as equable all year round. Even in Sicily, despite frequent blue skies, they have frosts and snow; and winter in the north of the country is usually more extreme than in Britain with more or

The Vespa – *literally, 'Wasp' – an Italian invention that suits the climate and way of life perfectly.*

Venetian gondolas have been painted black since a 16th-century law forbade excessive displays of wealth. It is also said that they are mourning the plague of 1630, which killed 50,000 people, reducing the city's population by a third.

less constant freezing fog in the plains from November to March. There are often torrential rains in spring and autumn, and the heat of summer can be stifling: humid in the North, dry and windswept by the irritating sirocco in the South.

The lakes, therefore, are a good place to start, and there can be few more delightful first images of Italy than the terraced slopes of the Borromean Islands on Lake Maggiore, ornamented with statues, palm trees, cypresses and wisteria, greeting you as you wake from a night on the train. Each of the lakes offers the magical combination of mountains and large expanses of water, lush vegetation and prettily sited towns and villages. Most have steamers and hydrofoils crossing from east to west and north to south during the summer months, and the tourist facilities – hotels, restaurants, cafés, beaches, campsites and windsurfing – are excellent, without spoiling the natural beauty of the surroundings.

The country and the city

South of the lakes, between the Alps and the Apennines, lies a string of historic cities. Every 20 to 30 miles you find one, each with its own architectural style, colours, atmosphere and personality. The sheer number of them is astonishing – though less so when you look at the history of the region.

Traditionally, the countryside of northern Italy was organised around its cities, in a series of concentric rings: first came the city ramparts, with market gardens and vineyards at their feet stretching out to arable fields and finally pastures. Geographers explain the predominance of towns by the contours of the landscape: the juxtaposition of hills and plains gave rise to conflicts between herdsmen and farmers, giving the inhabitants of the towns the position of arbiters. Other authorities have a different theory: they see Rome as the

key factor and argue that towns developed around Roman camps along the great roads – such as the Via Aurelia, which went from Rome to modern Marseille.

Northern Italy saw the birth of the first city communes in modern Europe, around the year AD 1000. They grew out of a long tradition of neighbourly solidarity, which can be seen in old Lombard customs such as the rule that a man could be held responsible for his neighbour's debts, or that, at funerals, the coffin bearers should be neighbours rather than family. Gradually, the neighbourhoods grouped into federations or communes. It was a slow process, unhurried on by any great leader, but simply the gradual extension of a sense of interdependence. Some communes began to extend their territories until they were major international powers. In the course of a few centuries the greatest of them, Venice, built an empire that stretched from Lombardy to Cyprus and included the coast of Dalmatia, the Ionian Islands, the Peloponnese and much of the Aegean archipelago – all of which still bear unmistakable testimony, in their elegant architecture, to the Venetian presence.

Portraits of cities

Varied as they are, these northern cities complement one another like the parts of a body. The brain is Florence: the city which dominated Italy culturally before Piedmont united it administratively. Some scholars have even claimed that the Italian language was born there. Certainly, it is a language whose rules of grammar and vocabulary were not established by grammarians and bureaucrats, as any Italian will proudly tell you, but by poets, in particular, the Florentine Dante. The language really is poetic, full of supple grace and music.

Dante, born in 1265, was exiled from his native city for political reasons from 1301 until his death 20 years later. He was famous for his eloquence, a gift with words that comes out clearly in his writings. In his masterpiece, *The Divine Comedy,* he places this chilling inscription over the gateway to hell:

The Italians' instinctive sense of posture – as well as their love of companionship – can be seen even when they ride bicycles. You often see a friend or younger brother standing statuesquely on the back while the other pedals.

St Mark's Square, Venice, on a summer afternoon, retains its magic despite mass invasions by tourists. In the background rises the façade of St Mark's Basilica, with a corner of the Doge's Palace to the right .

The finely wrought tail end of a gondola. Sadly, these wonderful 'water cabs' are rarely used by anyone other than tourists nowadays. The more usual form of transport is the vaporetto, *or water bus.*

Italy has catapulted itself from one of the poorest nations of Europe to one of the richest in the space of thirty years. These diners exude the confident aplomb of the wealthy.

Per me si va nella città dolente,
Per me si va nell' eterno dolore,
Per me si va tra la perduta gente ...
Lasciate ogni speranza voi ch' entrate.

Through me you go into the city of grief,
Through me you go into eternal pain,
Through me you go among the lost people ...
Abandon all hope, you who enter here.

The lines are unforgettable, and still manage to send a shiver down the spine in a secular, scientific age which has long since ceased to believe in the literal existence of hell.

The Florentines had an influence on other aspects of life besides the language: their authority was even greater in the matter of colours and forms. The legislators here were the artists and architects of the early Renaissance such as Masaccio, Donatello and Brunelleschi. In their revival of classical Greek and Roman principles of design, combined with the parallel efforts of humanist philosophers and scholars, they brought about the biggest change in Western thought and perception since the coming of Christianity. Later, Florence was also the native city of two of the three giants of the late Renaissance – Michelangelo and Leonardo da Vinci – while the third, Raphael, spent many of his most productive years there.

To appreciate the Florentines' genius, you have only to look at the majestic cathedral complex in their city. In this remarkable building, massive stone structures are so perfectly proportioned that they appear almost to be weightless and float in the air – an impression enhanced by the use of coloured marble and terracotta to create an

exquisite visual harmony. Brunelleschi's dome, built in 1420-36, was at the time of its construction the largest in the world.

You find the same coherence and balance in the Florentines themselves: they are calm, logical and realistic, and their utter lack of whimsy and sentimentality can make them seem almost too cerebral (Machiavelli, the most brutally clear-headed of all political thinkers, was a Florentine). But they also have a saving gift of irony and humour, with considerable reserves of passion beneath their polished manners.

If Florence is the brain of Italy, Venice is the eye – a liquid film reflecting images of fabulous vanished ages: golden cupolas, Byzantine mosaics and Gothic traceries

in stone. The exotic feeling is particularly strong when you arrive by sea: the scintillating domes of St Mark, the bell towers like minarets, and everything suggesting Byzantium and the East. In fact, Venice seems like a highly coloured piece of Asia that has broken away and drifted up to the northern end of the Adriatic. At the height of its glory – and, for all Florence's artistic achievements, Venice was the power with greater economic and political clout – it must have seemed like a pirate's lair, with gold from India, Chinese silks and oriental spices, furniture, sculpture and architectural fragments bought or pillaged from the four corners of the Earth. Now that time has laid its patina on what remains, everything in this great treasure house seems natural and fitting, and the winged lions of St Mark's Square, which came originally from the ruins of Mesopotamia, look as if they were born on one of the islands of the Venetian lagoon.

What is Venice's secret? First, wherever you are in Venice, your eye never falls on anything ugly: the houses, the bridges, the street lamps, even the door bells are works of art. The most ordinary everyday objects are somehow transfigured. Look at the dustmen's boats surging through the canals, piled high with mounds of rubbish – they look like something painted by Canaletto. Secondly, space is beautifully organised in Venice, with even the most public places having an intimate feel. The square in front of the Fenice opera house is like a

The surreal effects of a city built on water are intensified at carnival time, when the bizarre, the sinister, the elegant and the whimsical meet to create dreamlike scenes.

The Po plain is not especially fertile, but it has reached a high level of prosperity due to intensive farming and to the numerous cities which offer markets for its produce. Despite the availability of all the latest agricultural technology, you can still find scenes like this if you travel off the beaten track.

A rare sight in modern Italy, where 90 per cent of homes have washing machines (compared to 4 per cent in 1953).

drawing-room, the streets like passageways to other rooms in a palace. Thirdly, there are no cars. And fourthly, the city is both small and more-or-less circular, which means that you never get seriously lost; if you keep walking long enough you do not end up in a desolate suburb but – at the worst – where you started.

Finally there is the lagoon, which is present everywhere, both to sight and smell. The sea is the binding element of the city, feeding and shaping it: like some fantastic shellfish, Venice has lived by filtering the sea for centuries, taking only what it needs, patiently building and accumulating until it has created for itself a unique and completely harmonious structure.

Milan – Italy's mighty arm

Milan, the workshop of Italy, might be described as the arm. At first sight it is a distinctly unattractive city. Its buildings are dark, heavy, with the discreet, shuttered opulence of a wealthy bourgeoisie that arrived long ago and has nothing left to prove. Except in one or two special areas, such as the Galleria Vittorio Emanuele and the Brera district, you will not see the Milanese strolling about. They are too busy working. In the countless offices and workshops of the city, in the factories of the grimly industrial *periferia,* they are all at it: toiling, grafting and earning money, day and night.

When the Milanese stop working, it is often to start complaining – which they do with a certain pride. The substance of their complaint is that they are the nation's drudges and that everyone else is idle. This is a myth of course, but it sustains them and few Milanese would willingly change towns. They love their austere avenues and their scrappy *naviglio* – the canal which is Milan's consolation for being one of the few major European cities without a river or seaside location.

Life in the Po delta – a landscape of lonely fields and canals reclaimed from marshes – is a far cry from the sophistication of the cities.

Introduced to southern Italy by the Arabs, the lemon now grows in many parts of the country. Lemon juice is often used instead of vinegar in cooking.

Above all, the Milanese are loyal to their city because of its enormous creative vitality. Situated at the centre of the Po plain, at the crossroads of the north-south and east-west axes of communication, Milan is like a powerful pump, sucking in and pushing out trade, investment, ideas, products and designs to every corner of Italy. Over the centuries it has tapped the human and agricultural resources of Lombardy, building its fortune first on cloth, armaments and banking, and then on manufacturing, to which it later added publishing, fashion and furnishing – in short, all the things for which Italy is famous except cinema (which is based in Rome) and Fiat (which is in Turin). There are no geographical limits to Milan's potential growth and no physical obstacles to stop it spreading across the plain like an inkspot. It takes full advantage of this fact, gradually swallowing up the villages and towns around it.

The city has another, final, claim to fame – one of the best-known paintings in the world: Leonardo da Vinci's *Last Supper* on the walls of the refectory of the convent of Santa Maria delle Grazie. Painting it apparently cost Leonardo immense pains: he spent weeks trying to get exactly the right expression for Judas, the betrayer of Jesus, and is said to have deliberately left the face of Jesus himself unfinished because he did not believe he was worthy to paint the face of God. Tragically, the fresco has deteriorated badly over the centuries. Instead of applying his paint directly to the damp plaster, Leonardo used the technique known as *fresco secco*, normally employed only on wood panels, in order to get a more brilliant effect. The trouble was that the paint soon started to flake and has had to be restored, with varying success, many times since.

Moving south to Bologna, you reach the stomach of Italy. Known as *la Grassa* ('the Fat'), it is the nation's capital of good food and good living. Not content with the invention of *mortadella* (an extremely large salami) and *spaghetti al ragù* (better known outside Italy as

Joining the Piazza del Duomo to the Piazza della Scala in Milan is the Galleria Vittorio Emanuele, a covered arcade of cafés and high-quality shops where the Milanese can meet in all weathers.

spaghetti bolognaise), the cooks of Bologna are experts in the saucing and stuffing of every conceivable form of pasta. They can take a large part of the credit for making Italy a country where it is practically impossible to eat badly. The Italian writer Luigi Barzini explains this by pointing out that Italian cooking sets out from a position of respect for nature – unlike French cooking, for example, which depends on transforming and blending its natural ingredients to the point where they are often unrecognisable. In Italy, wine must taste of grapes, and meat must be lightly and simply cooked; it may even be served raw, as in the celebrated dish of *carpaccio.* A fresh dressing of lemon or olive oil, a few leaves of basil, some slivers of parmesan and the dish is ready: there are few disguises in Italian cuisine. To be fair to Bologna, the city and its people do other things besides eating, and they do them supremely well. Bologna is also known as *la Dotta* ('the Learned'): its university is the oldest in Europe, with a reputation for

scientific – particularly medical – excellence. It was the first university to permit dissection of human bodies, in the 14th century, and it numbers among its alumni Copernicus and the poets Petrarch and Dante. A third nickname for Bologna is *la Rossa* ('the Red'), which is apt in two ways: the city is built almost entirely of brick, and has been a traditional stronghold of Communism.

The heart of Italy

If Florence, Venice, Milan and Bologna are the head, eyes, arms and stomach, where is the heart of Italy? Here the choice becomes more difficult. Large cities such as Turin and Genoa are too industrial. The smaller but equally historic cities such as Verona, Padua, Ravenna, Siena, Bergamo or Pisa are probably more suitable, with Verona, scene of Shakespeare's *Romeo and Juliet,* as good a candidate as any.

The city is identified with these famous lovers as inevitably as Assisi is with St Francis. Verona also has a special geographical position, at the junction of mountains and plains, with Lake Garda – the largest of the Italian lakes – close by. Verona can make a rival claim to Milan as the 'crossroads' of northern Italy, sitting as it does on the direct route to Germany through the Brenner Pass. It is wonderfully gracious and a delight to walk around. In the cafés on its three most

beautiful squares, Piazza Brà, Piazza delle Erbe and Piazza dei Signori, the Italian art of living is practised to perfection. The city also boasts a cultural feast in the world-famous opera and ballet festival which takes place in July and August each year in the spectacularly dramatic setting of its huge Roman arena – Italy's second-largest after the Colosseum in Rome.

Padua might also be considered: bridgehead of the Venetian land empire and home of another venerable university (founded in 1222), whose students enliven in term time its quiet provincial charm. It also boasts the greatest cycle of frescoes by Giotto, in the famous Scrovegni Chapel.

A discussion in Italy is always accompanied by theatrical gestures and facial expressions. The man on the left clearly cannot see any sense in what the man on the right is trying so insistently to tell him.

Ravenna is a different sort of place altogether. It remained for centuries the last western redoubt of the Eastern Roman Empire, and it still feels like an outpost today. The glory of the town is its 6th-century Byzantine mosaics, which are the finest in Europe. Their blaze of colour lights up that obscure period of history between antiquity and the Middle Ages, when Roman civilisation became Christianised under the influence of the East.

Siena, too, is a serious candidate. It is a welcoming, friendly city where you immediately feel at home. It was a rival city-state to Florence for at least 400 years, but unlike Florence it has had the good fortune this century to escape the worst consequences of mass tourism. The rust-red earth of the surrounding country was used to make a pigment, known as *sienna* (raw or burnt); yet the most memorable colours of the city are the black and white marble of its cathedral and the vivid yellows, blues and reds of the banners and Renaissance costumes displayed at the annual *palio*. This event, a horse race held in the main square on July 2 and August 16 each year, is one of the most spectacular in Italy.

The leaning tower of Pisa was once used by Galileo for experiments with gravity, and is now used by

Loved, venerated and exploited, the mother is the linchpin of the Italian family – some would say of the whole of Italian society.

A street in the Cinque Terre. Set among coastal cliffs east of Genoa, these villages have been protected by their inaccessible position from the intensive tourist development that has taken place along the Ligurian shore.

The fishing port of Camogli, between Genoa and Portofino, was once famous for its merchant ships. It is now best known for its colourful festivals: the Blessing of the Fish in May, and the Stella Maris, a procession of fishing boats, in August.

The gecko, a lizard 6 to 12 inches long, is found all over Italy. Harmless to humans, it does useful service in eating troublesome insects.

tourists for trick photographs. But there is much more to the city than its tower. The architecture of the tower, and indeed of the whole cathedral area to which it belongs, is dazzling even by Italian standards. In the Middle Ages, Pisa was a powerful maritime republic whose territories included Corsica, Sardinia and the Balearic Islands, and its wealth is reflected in the religious buildings and imposing palazzi of the town.

Parma, too, is a candidate: the birthplace of the conductor Toscanini and of Italy's most successful cheese, *parmigiano*. Then there is Ferrara, whose Castello Estense stands as a memorial to one of the

great Renaissance courts of Europe; and of course Bergamo, Vicenza, Urbino, Pavia, Mantua ... the choice is bewildering.

Vicenza, in particular, has a special claim to fame. It was the birthplace in 1508 of one of the most influential architects in history: Andrea di Pietro, better known by his nickname Palladio. In works such as *The Four Books on Architecture (I Quattro Libri dell' Architettura)*, published in 1570 and translated into most European languages, Palladio helped to introduce a new style based on the classical style of ancient Rome. It influenced architecture for centuries to come – particularly in England and America. Vicenza proudly names its main street, the Corso Palladio, after him and has one of his masterpieces in the Basilica – a 15th-century city hall which he reclothed with a two-storey classical arcade in dazzling white stone. Just outside the city is another of his most famous works: the severely symmetrical Villa Rotunda, inspiration for numerous buildings in succeeding centuries, including Thomas Jefferson's Monticello in Virginia.

The primacy of Italy's cities does not mean that the countryside has been neglected or destroyed. Right

A Tuscan villa-farmhouse rises proudly from its hilltop. Such glorious homes seem to sum up the classical beauty of the region's rich cultural traditions. Small wonder that they have become so popular with well-to-do foreigners seeking a gracious second home in the sun.

along the Alpine arc there are landscapes of unspoilt grandeur: the Dolomites, the Brenta massif and the Val d'Aosta. Farther south you still find oases of wilderness such as the Cinque Terre ('the Five Lands'). This stretch of the Ligurian coast has always been difficult to reach, and is protected on the shore side by steep cliffs. Despite its popularity with holidaymakers, there is simply nowhere for development to occur and so, as a result, the five small towns of the Cinque Terre – Monterosso al Mare, Vernazza, Corniglia, Manarola and Riomaggiore – retain their beauty. Even Tuscany ('Chianti-shire' to the English) has hills and forests where the marks of man are scarce.

Asti, once a powerful Piedmontese city, is known today principally for its wines. Harvest time is marked by festivals where you can taste the produce: not just the sweet Asti Spumante but also excellent red wines such as Barolo and Barbaresco.

Apart from these rare exceptions, the landscape of Italy has been ceaselessly worked by farmers. From the Alps in the north to Mount Etna on Sicily in the south, hills and plains have been cleared, tilled, terraced, divided, drained and generally remodelled over countless generations. Everywhere you see walls, irrigation channels, aqueducts, farm buildings and houses built from all sorts of materials: slate, brick, sandstone, terracotta, timber, iron and marble. The result is a more complete harmony between buildings and their environment than you will find perhaps anywhere else in the world.

A village house in the Abruzzi mountains east of Rome. Local traditions are still strong here, but note too the TV aerials and the Christmas tree outside the front door.

A state of grace

Who are the inhabitants, as well as the architects, of these marvellous places? The first thing to note is that in Italy appearances are not deceptive. They are the real thing. Look at a typical Italian, man or woman: how they stand, with the self-possession of an actor on the stage, happy to be the focus of all eyes. There is no affectation about it, just what one might call a naturally theatrical presence. For the Italians inhabit their bodies gracefully, and learn to do so from an early age. Foreign observers have noted that the 'awkward age' of

adolescence scarcely exists in Italy: the children are like little grown-ups, courteous, well dressed and clean. The familiar Northern European figure of the gawky, pustular teenager with a permanent chip on his shoulder is practically unknown. Italians pass smoothly from childhood to adulthood, and then smoothly again from adulthood to old age. They have a trick of making light of their troubles and appearing to lead a charmed existence.

If it is possible to generalise about an entire nation, they are extremely good-looking: lovely eyes and beautifully poised figures in the women; chiselled medallion features and wiry, nervous grace in the men. A good three-quarters of them look as if they have stepped out of paintings by Raphael or Botticelli. Even the plain-looking – who of course exist – have the vivacious, happy-go-lucky expressions of characters in the traditional, improvised comedy dramas of the *Commedia dell'Arte.*

The Italians get their marvellous gift of physical ease partly from the way they care about their own appearance: they are scrupulously clean, spend as much as they can afford on clothes and work hard on the detail – trousers immaculately pressed, colours right, hair perfectly groomed. But there is a deeper reason too. The Italians live at peace with their bodies, making the best of them, without being neurotic. What they want out of life is happiness and, to an Italian, looking good is feeling good.

Of course not all of them succeed and Italy has its fair share of misfits, neurotics, depressives and no-hopers (they are, after all, human). In Milan and Rome, as in all big Western cities of today, psychiatrists have more work than they can handle. Yet, when all is said and done, the Italians have a capacity for sheer effusive gaiety that is rare in the world. Go to a cinema on a Sunday afternoon, or a football match down at the *stadio,* or a village festival, and you can feel it, crackling like static through the air.

There have been many attempts at explaining the state of grace that the Italians seem uniquely to inhabit. The 19th-century French historian Hippolyte Taine wrote: 'The Italian is not susceptible to bare ideas. He finds he has to clothe them in some palpable form.' A similar idea occurred, somewhat more memorably, to his countryman, the poet Henri de Régnier: 'The Frenchman sings badly and thinks well, the German sings well and thinks badly, the Italian doesn't think, he just sings!' Earlier, an Italian travelling companion of

Lunch in the Veneto countryside. The family are eagerly eyeing the pot of polenta, *a corn semolina that was once the staple diet of the peasantry in this part of the country. It is now served as an accompaniment to much richer fare.*

A Tuscan woman carries a pot of coals which she will use to warm the beds. Winter is often colder here than in Britain.

the German poet Goethe expressed a similar thought: 'Why think? It makes you old. A man must have his head full of things, all in great confusion!' In the Italian scale of values, vitality, passion and the love of beauty come before everything else.

The sense of beauty is crucial, for what is the privileged domain of a select few in most countries belongs to everyone in Italy. When the Italians are not busy making beautiful things they are busy buying them. The walls of sitting rooms and restaurants across the nation are covered in pictures – real oils and watercolours incidentally, not reproductions. In the smallest provincial town you will find picture auctions

and exhibitions, and they will be attended by ordinary working people.

There is, necessarily, a negative side to all this vitality, this cult of feeling and looking good. The same urge that drives the Italians to make everything a work of art also drives them away from the more routine tasks of life. The craftsman may be happy hammering copper, forging iron, making mosaics, blowing glass, or carving wood, but those in less creative jobs may find their work less satisfying. For the bank clerk, the doctor in the casualty department, the public administrator (unless he is a Communist keen to prove a point) it can be harder to find pleasure in doing a job well.

Bringing in the hay from the high mountain meadows of the Dolomites. In the background rise some of the dramatic, rocky peaks that are characteristic of the range.

Chaos and initiative

The Italians' dislike of collective discipline and regulation is seen most flagrantly in their driving manners. The most basic rules of the road are systematically disobeyed. Traffic lights, speed limits and one-way signs are ignored; indicators are not used; cars overtake on the inside, park anywhere, and will even drive murderously along pavements to get round traffic queues. (All of this is standard in Rome and farther south; somewhat less so in the North.) Drivers brought up in more orderly climes are torn between fury and incredulity at these antics. Oddly enough, though,

the Italians have fewer serious road accidents than the French, Germans or British: no doubt because they are more skilful drivers, with reactions necessarily honed to lightning speed by the chaos in the streets.

All the faults, large and small, of social life in Italy are made tolerable by the problem-solving, improvisatory flair and straightforward kindness of individual people. There is a way around just about any obstacle; the trick is to find it. The Italians do this by discussing the problem, circling it, examining it, questioning, and worrying at it until it cracks.

Anyone who stays in Italy for a while will inevitably come up against the state bureaucracy sooner or later: forms and certificates which are necessary but unobtainable, procedures that seem designed purely to waste time, complicated administrative dilemmas that cannot be solved through normal channels. Occasionally, as you watch a whole morning evaporate in the quest for some ludicrous piece of paper, the thought may occur to you that the purpose of these obstructive practices is none other than to enable the official in charge to personalise his service by making a heroic gesture of rescue. He may soften at the sight of the child crying by your side, or be impressed by the fact you come *raccomandato* by the friend of a friend, or

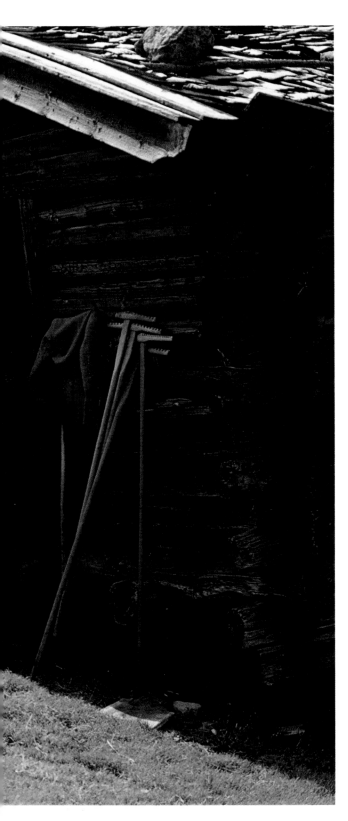

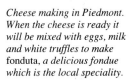

Cheese making in Piedmont. When the cheese is ready it will be mixed with eggs, milk and white truffles to make fonduta, *a delicious fondue which is the local speciality.*

simply be touched by your despairing smile. The result, in any case, is like magic. A 'grave and irregular situation' suddenly becomes a matter of no importance, a solution is found, the Gordian knot is cut. This even applies to the police. Under every uniform there is a human being waiting to enhance his personal prestige by doing you a favour. All you have to do is ask in a friendly way.

When all these personal favours and special exceptions are added together, the inevitable follows: violation of a host of laws, fiscal fraud, uncontrolled building development, and failures and inefficiencies in public services. To balance this, it has to be said that a certain degree of disorder, which would be regarded as intolerable by an Englishman or German, is accepted by the Italians. In fact, they think of it as a guarantee of liberty, since it allows local and individual initiatives to come into play. It also allows the existence of Italy's vast black economy, thousands of small family or one-man enterprises which do all their business in cash and bypass the red tape of the state altogether. Even public servants take part: they finish work at lunchtime and go off to a second, private job in the afternoon.

This 'black' economy, which governments are careful not to obstruct too completely, owes its vitality to the deeper forms of solidarity that exist in Italian society: family, friends and neighbours. The state and large enterprises are generally regarded with mistrust, while small productive companies run by cousins or people in the village are valued as family affairs, where people are themselves and not just a number.

Looking at the broader picture of society as a whole, it is tempting to talk of waste, 'lack of public spirit' and so on. But before reaching for these terms of condemnation it is worth stopping to ask why this informal, family-based system has survived so long and remains so dynamic and healthy. One crucial reason is that Italians generally limit their horizons: they reserve their trust and affection for those around them, the people they know. Everyone else they politely ignore.

A carnival costume with a difference ... This crafty Venetian citizen is managing to beat the acqua alta, *when the lagoon floods the city, without spoiling his festive attire.*

The Splendour and Misery of the South

South of Tuscany a different Italy begins: less active, less open and less wealthy. The transition is not abrupt, though, for the region of Umbria provides a buffer zone. Umbria is not exactly poor: the houses are pretty, the vineyards plentiful, the fields fertile and well-maintained; and the soil looks rich and well capable of supporting life.

But what was good enough to fend off famine in the Middle Ages is not enough to keep people on the land today. Compared with its northern neighbours, Umbria has very little industry. Having missed the industrial revolution, Umbria also missed the handouts of the *Cassa per il Mezzogiorno*, a state fund offering economic aid to the backward South of the country. As soon as you enter Umbria, you feel the change. You have left the Italy that is up-to-date with everything else in the world for a land where history came to a halt long ago. Judging by the architecture of the towns, that moment was some time in the Middle Ages. Circled by ramparts and crisscrossed by narrow streets, these places have scarcely changed in 700 years.

The most striking of the medieval cities is Assisi, where everything seems to date from the 13th century, the time of St Francis. The paved streets twist crookedly between house fronts bulging with age. Even the birds, to whom St Francis preached a famous sermon, seem to be present in unusual numbers, strutting along the town's pink ramparts undisturbed. In its perfect marriage of architecture, landscape and light, Assisi's unchanging charm provides a powerful reinforcement to its attraction as a centre of pilgrimage.

The other cities of Umbria lack the spiritual appeal of Assisi, although many are just as lovely to the eye. Perched on hilltops or rocky crags, the towns of Orvieto, Gubbio, Montefalco and Spoleto look out over rolling landscapes of fields, rivers and lakes, a faint, misty quality to the light softening every line. Even Perugia, the capital, whose history goes back to the Etruscans (rulers of much of central Italy before the Romans overcame them in the 5th century BC), manages to float superbly clear of the industrial suburbs clustered around its base.

Appropriately labelled 'the green heart of Italy' by the tourist brochures, Umbria offers much more than its historic towns. The countryside is peaceful, its gentle hills planted with olives and pines. There is Lake Trasimeno, and an endless variety of spas, known all over Italy for their mineral waters. Most famous is San Gemini, known for its table water, while others are recommended for specific medical conditions: Furapane and Massa Martana for liver and digestive complaints; Fontecchio for rheumatism; Nocera Umbra for dyspepsia and gastritis.

Beyond Umbria lies Rome, a metropolis which already had over a million inhabitants at the time of the birth of Christ. To those who view it today – a city that overwhelms the visitor with the glory of its past – it is salutary to remember that Rome has not always been so powerful or so densely populated. In the 6th and 7th centuries, following the barbarian invasions, there were no more than 15,000 inhabitants, grazing their pigs and chickens among the ruins of what had once been the capital of the world.

To put itself back on the map, Rome has had to smother most of the surrounding communities and countryside. Its modern suburbs – the *periferia* – are notoriously depressing. Yet there are oases of beauty, where the great Roman families built their country retreats. Notable among these are Albano, Castel Gandolfo (where the Pope stays in summer), Ariccia, Nemi, Rocca di Papa, Frascati and, best of all, Tivoli, with the dazzling water gardens of the Villa d'Este and the haunting remains of Hadrian's Villa.

Pope Pius II, visiting in 1461, described Hadrian's Villa in these terms: 'Time has ruined all; ivy covers the walls that once were clothed with tapestries and golden draperies; thorns and scrub flourish where once sat purple-clad tribunes, and snakes infest the queen's chambers: such is the transient lot of human affairs.' A similar sentiment is apt to make itself felt the farther south you travel.

The Via San Giacomo in Assisi is one of many streets in this Umbrian city which have hardly changed since the time of St Francis.

The eternal city

The city of Rome fills many people with trepidation. The sheer weight of history, present in every stone, bewilders the imagination. The best advice for visitors is to decide at once which Rome to see, and to ignore the rest. This may seem brutal, but it is the only way to avoid serious mental indigestion.

If your interest is in antiquity, you should go straight to the Forum, with its symbols of imperial victory now pleasantly softened by time, and its ruined temples to Saturn, Mars, Castor and Pollux, and Vesta. Amongst the broken columns and crooked paving stones, ancient Rome seems very real. It is easy to imagine the passing chariots, the lictors, the senators hurrying to the Capitol, and the triumphal processions of victorious generals. Just down the road is the Colosseum, which was built in the 1st century AD as a stadium where the gory popular entertainments included gladiators and mock sea battles for 50,000 spectators.

If, on the other hand, you prefer papal Rome, you should head for the massive fortress of Castel Sant'Angelo. Originally designed as a mausoleum for the Emperor Hadrian, it became the citadel of the popes in the Middle Ages, and later a prison and cannon foundry. Since the beginning of this century it has been a museum. From here it is a short walk to St Peter's Square with its great embracing colonnade, where Christians gather from all over the world to be blessed by the Pope. It was on this spot that St Peter, the first Bishop of Rome, was martyred around AD 67. After visiting the basilica and the Vatican museum, you can continue your tour of papal Rome by wandering around the city centre, noting how many hundreds of monuments, plaques, churches, palaces and fountains were erected by the various popes at the height of their earthly power.

The story does not end with the popes, however. There is also early Christian Rome, with its catacombs and churches glittering with mosaics. Other periods too left their mark, not all of them to Rome's advantage. Mussolini's triumphal route of the Via dei Fori Imperiali is generally regarded as a travesty, as is the late 19th-century monument to King Victor Emmanuel II – a gigantic white marble structure of unforgettable vulgarity, known jokingly to Romans as 'the wedding cake' or 'the typewriter'.

This division into 'periods' belies the situation on the ground. Ancient, medieval, Renaissance, baroque, neo-classical and modern stand side by side, if not actually on top of one another. St Peter's is built on the gardens of Nero's Circus; the President of the Republic lives in the Quirinal Palace, which was previously the official residence of the King and, for almost 300 years before that (1592-1870), of the popes. A baroque façade covers a medieval interior; a classical column is built into a row of 15th-century houses; and an ancient Roman prison is turned into the crypt of a church.

The Romans threw nothing away, recycling parts of old buildings to make new ones. Even the Colosseum, whose sheer size pronounced it an architectural masterpiece, was quarried mercilessly for iron and stone throughout the Middle Ages.

The art of remodelling ancient materials was taken to extreme lengths by Pope Pius IX, who in 1860 commissioned a sculptor to modify certain of the statues in the Villa Borghese gardens. Caius Gracchus, a reformer and champion of the underprivileged in the 2nd century BC, had his hair removed and several lines added to his face in order to transform him into the 1st-century architect Vitruvius; and Savonarola (1452-98), a much later reformer, was converted into the 11th-century musical theorist Guido d'Arezzo by the skilful adaptation of a Dominican habit.

Carabinieri in Rome. Officially part of the army, the carabinieri *are the main police force, and provide a guard for the most important public buildings in cities.*

The result of these perpetual absorptions, additions and modifications might have been an unbearable clutter – but it rarely reaches that point. More often the effect is one of magnificent profusion. The reason is that most of Rome's buildings and monuments were designed by the greatest architects and sculptors of their day, people whose technique was based on the study of the classical models that the city so abundantly provided. They seldom put a foot wrong.

Of all these great figures, one of the very greatest was undoubtedly Michelangelo, who left his mark as sculptor, architect and painter. His most famous sculptural work in the city is also one of his earliest, the *Pietà* which now confronts you on the right as you enter St Peter's – he finished it when he was still just 25 years old. His friend, the banker Jacopo Galli who won him the commission, promised that the sculpture would be 'the most beautiful work in marble in Rome today'. It was, and for many people still is – a truly sublime work in its depiction of the Virgin Mary grieving over the dead body of Christ.

Michelangelo's other contribution to St Peter's started just under half a century later. In 1546, by now famous throughout Italy and beyond, he took over as the architect in charge of rebuilding the basilica – in place of the original one (which had dated in part from the 4th century AD). In fact, he was just one among a succession of architects, both before and after him, who were entrusted with the task, and his plans for the building were later overlaid with the brasher, baroque St Peter's of today. Even his mighty dome was modified in the construction – which does not prevent it from being an awesome creation. The gallery running around its inner rim still offers some of the best, if dizzying, views of the nave 250 feet below and the high altar with its

ornate bronze *baldachino* (canopy). An outside balcony, meanwhile, reveals equally stunning views over the Vatican rooftops and towards the Gianicolo Hill.

But, of course, Michelangelo's greatest works by far in Rome are his frescoes in the Vatican's Sistine Chapel: the depiction of the Creation on the ceiling and the Last Judgment on the rear wall. The artist, a dogmatic and often difficult man in his own right, was forced unwillingly into this task by the equally authoritarian Pope Julius II. It was a stormy relationship, though eventually a fruitful one. To paint the ceiling, whose centrepiece is the famous representation of God bringing Adam to life, Michelangelo had to spend four years lying on his back on scaffolding. He refused to allow any assistants to help him, so that the finished product is all his own.

The Spanish Steps in Rome lead from the Piazza di Spagna to the church of Trinità dei Monti. The poet Keats died in a little house on the right in February 1821; the house is now a museum.

Dinner in Trastevere, once a poor quarter of Rome, but now highly fashionable. The streets radiating from Piazza Santa Maria have some of Rome's most popular restaurants.

Rome and the Romans

Another factor that makes Rome's rich layer cake of history work so well is that its people treat their city with such casual abandon. Traffic roars around the Colosseum; pedlars set up their stalls outside the most prestigious churches; and baroque courtyards are used for parking. Yet if this seems sacrilegious, the opposite would be even more shocking: Rome's monuments all roped off or surrounded by immaculate lawns and metal barriers. That would drain both the monuments and the city of life, and turn the centre of Rome into no more than a tourist ghetto.

The strength of Rome lies in its power to absorb monuments and tourists into its own buzzing, dynamic life, so that the past is connected with the present and kept alive. Things carry on as they always have done, with trinkets being sold at the doors of temples, rubbish piled up outside the most beautiful villas, and dogs lifting their legs on the corners of palaces. It may be annoying at times, but it is also a sure sign that the Eternal City is still itself, that its people are still there, working, eating and enjoying themselves. If motorbikes

clutter an arched entrance once intended for a coach and pair, or if posters splash gaudy colours across a sober Renaissance façade, no one minds. Works of art are so plentiful here that the Romans would not be able to move if they respected them all. So they prefer to treat them with nonchalance and familiarity instead – rather like the South American Indian children who so nonplussed the conquistadores by using nuggets of gold as toys.

There is a time – at night – though, when the clamour of Rome dies down and you can feel the ghostly presence of the centuries in the silence around you. Roman nights have a unique charm. This is partly because of the mild climate, which draws you out of doors at all times of year, but it also has to do with the quality of the light and darkness. Unlike the uniform sodium glare of British street lighting, the street lamps of Rome cast a theatrical, magical light: a splash of white on the pavement, a little on the lower walls, and darkness on the upper floors. The lights are irregularly placed – between one and the next there are often pools of darkness. Yet the haphazard succession of light and dark creates intriguing patterns that spark the

The farther south you go in Italy, the deeper the social divisions between men and women. With lunch over, the men stay at table discussing football or politics while the women are clearing up inside.

A street stall selling drinks in Naples. Notice how beautifully the stall is 'dressed' with lemons and pitchers.

Naples, a city where everything is out in the open ... The Neapolitans share their sorrows and joys – and washing lines – with both family and neighbours.

One of the conically roofed houses known as trulli, *which dot the countryside around Alberobello in the south-eastern region of Puglia.*

The onion harvest in Calabria. Despite massive state investment, the South of Italy remains far poorer than the North.

imagination, inflame curiosity, and lead the walker on, despite the late hour, to unplanned hikes across the city. There is really no such thing, in Rome, as a short after-dinner walk.

See Naples and die

Only two hours down the *autostrada* from Rome, Naples is like a city from a different universe. Whereas Rome lives in the light of eternity, Naples takes each day as it comes, as if there were no yesterday or tomorrow – only a constant, feverish search for happiness in the passing moment.

The first impression of Naples is of a colourful,

realise that you would be better off without the car. You should, though, resist the temptation to triple-park or leave your car on a pavement. Everyone else does it, of course, and the police do not seem to care, but you risk never seeing it again. Naples is notorious for its thieves. There is a famous story of a cruiser that came into the bay one evening in 1945. As the ship dropped anchor, a launch approached and a smartly uniformed official came on board to inform the captain that quarantine regulations required the entire crew to go ashore for the night. The captain did as he was told, and found the next morning that his ship had disappeared – as, of course, had the 'official'. The vessel was never seen again, although a few weeks later a section of hull-plating turned up in a scrapyard several miles down the coast, with three or four letters of the ship's name still visible.

Making ricotta, *a soft white curd cheese much used in cooking. It is always made with sheep's milk.*

ragged and startling place. As soon as you arrive, look up at the windows and you will notice the city's traditional banners – trousers, dresses and shirts, drying in the wind. The streets below are filled with the sounds of traffic, klaxons, squealing brakes, skidding tyres, and the shouts and songs of the Neapolitans as they go about their business or indulge in the pleasures of the *struscio*. This word (pronounced 'strroosho' and meaning, literally, 'rub, chafe') suggests perfectly the murmur of scuffling feet and bodies endlessly brushing past one another in the river of humanity that flows interminably through the city.

After driving around for a while amongst wheezing automobiles, open-air workshops, street stalls, card players, and children playing football with old tins, you

Once you have parked your car safely, and made sure that you are not carrying a handbag or any obvious purse, wallet or expensive jewellery, you can set off to discover the city. Be prepared for a series of surprises. The first is the architecture. The houses are built largely of *tufo,* an easily worked stone, and have an astonishing variety of façades. Some look like great church organs, others like Viennese pastries. The view from the internal courtyards is even more surprising, with the staircases spiralling dizzily up, crossing landings and catwalks that are so flimsy they seem to tremble in the slightest breeze. There is usually little to see inside the houses except small, dark rooms. Go down to the basement, however, and with luck you will get a glimpse of the vast network of caves which lies under the streets of Naples.

The second surprise is the Neapolitans themselves. They are known the world over as singers and cooks, inventors of *bel canto* and pizza, as well as thieves and tricksters par excellence. There is much more to them than this, however. They are a people haunted by life and death. Death sits brooding over the city in the shape of Mount Vesuvius, the volcano that destroyed nearby Pompeii and Herculaneum in AD 79 and has continued to erupt at irregular intervals ever since. There are also earthquakes which periodically ravage the area, the last one in 1980. Death is ever-present on a more intimate scale, too, with the coffin-makers' workshops in the streets and the pomp and glory of traditional Neapolitan funerals passing by.

Perhaps because of the menace of Vesuvius and these reminders of death everywhere, life goes on with fantastic exuberance. The festivals of Naples are spectacular, especially at Easter, with the *via crucis* ('way of the cross') on the island of Procida, the feast of the Madonna dell'Arco, and the time on Easter Monday when tens of thousands of pilgrims gather on the slopes of Vesuvius. September has the most festivals: in the first week, anyone who wants to be cured of the curse of the evil eye goes to Mount Partenio; on the 19th there is the annual ceremony of the liquefaction of the blood of St Januarius, an occasion for extraordinary mass

Italian streets, particularly narrow ones in old cities, often lack pavements. This can give the pedestrian the impression that the whole street belongs to him – until a car comes along and he finds that none of it does.

demonstrations of faith. Perhaps the most spectacular of all the Neapolitan feasts is Santa Maria del Carmine, on July 16. If you happen to arrive in Naples on that day you may be forgiven for thinking the city is about to suffer the same fate as Pompeii, as flashes fill the sky and the buildings shake to the thud of explosions. It is only a fireworks display, of course, but on such a gigantic scale that it seems more like war or Vesuvius attempting to blow itself to bits.

Naples was once the largest port in the Mediterranean, and is still the third biggest city in Italy – after Rome and Milan, which overtook Naples at the end of the 19th century. It is a huge commercial and industrial centre. Naturally, not all the commercial activity is legal. Secret gambling dens, brothels and illicit trade of every description feed a large proportion of the city's 2 million inhabitants. When the customs make one of their periodic attempts to stop the flow of contraband into and out of Naples, there are massive popular protests and demonstrations. The *carabinieri* scarcely do any better in their struggles against the

camorra – the Neapolitan version of the Mafia. They make spectacular waves of arrests, which may include the arrests of policemen, magistrates and nuns, as well as more conventional criminals; and there is a moment of shock and disruption. Then life settles down again to its normal pace – and the corruption, property speculation and trafficking continue. Since this tradition

A typical southern hilltop town, its houses looking as if they have been cut directly from the rock.

In the poor, stark world of the Mezzogiorno *(the South), the simplest things can create an effect of beauty or magic.*

is older than any of the institutions set up to combat it –
it goes back to the time when Naples was run by
Spanish viceroys as a virtual private estate – most
people simply shrug their shoulders and accept it as an
inevitable part of life.

The Neapolitans are philosophical about most things.
They have a tolerant, accommodating attitude to their
fellow human beings. In this sense, among others, one
might well regard Naples as the heart of Italy.

Into the deep South

The farther south you travel, the poorer Italy becomes.
This is the general rule, although certain oases stand
out. Among these are Pompeii and the Amalfi coast.
Pompeii is a reminder of the splendour of imperial
Rome, a glimpse of life almost 2000 years ago. The

*A room in the cave-like
houses of Matera, many of
which have now been
abandoned. The town is the
capital of the Basilicata
region.*

*A trullo at Alberobello in
Puglia. Trulli are built with
stones that have been cleared
from the fields; their conical
roofs are laid without mortar.*

paved, rectilinear streets were bordered with shops and
rich houses, temples and brothels. Pompeii was once a
holiday town for Romans, a smart and lively resort of
some 25,000 inhabitants; the frescoes in the houses are
vivid and still colourful. Then, in AD 79, the
catastrophic eruption of Vesuvius belched out choking
vapours and a sudden cascade of ash and stones over the
city, burying it 20 feet deep. The bodies of animals and
humans, discovered 18 centuries later, have a disturbing
intimacy about them, as if they were neighbours.

The Amalfi coast is an oasis of a different kind: an
outcrop of luxury in an area where poverty seems the
norm. It was the same in the ancient world, when
emperors and patricians built sumptuous villas here.
Later, they were replaced by Roman prelates, and in the
last century by English aristocrats. Since the 1960s the
international jet set have made this coast, from Sorrento
to Maiori, one of their favourite stopping places.
Curiously enough, it would be hard to imagine a less
welcoming landscape: 30 miles of rocky cliffs plunging

into the sea, interrupted by jagged inlets and coves.
Every mile or so, however, a town opens out like a
painter's dream: Maiori, set among lemon trees;
Ravello, like a lovely balcony over the water; Amalfi,
with its white houses huddled against the rock;
Positano; Sorrento ... the names alone are enough to set
one yearning.

After this short taste of paradise, the descent towards
absolute poverty begins again. Empty roads wind off
across a landscape made desolate by the sun, through
villages of grey houses inhabited by old men and
women in black. Basilicata and Calabria: these are
regions of a primitive, neglected and underdeveloped
world. It seems a strange destiny for an area that was
once, as a part of Magna Graecia, a centre of ancient
Greek civilisation. It was here that Pythagoras lived and
worked, where precious metals mined in central Italy
were stored for shipping and sale, and where prosperous
farms chequered the countryside around the great cities
of Metapontum, Croton, Tarentum, Sybaris and
Heraclea.

For a few centuries before the birth of Christ, history
favoured these places, then abandoned them utterly. So
complete is the decline that in some cases one begins to
wonder whether ancient historians were telling the
truth. They say, for example, that Sybaris, the
richest of the Greek colonial cities (and the origin of the
term sybaritic, denoting extreme luxury), stood at the
mouth of the Coscile. Yet nothing now remains except
sandbanks and water.

Nature, at least, has changed little in these parts. The fields of Puglia are still lush with wheat, vines and olives; citrus trees still crowd the Calabrian coast; and, inland, the Sila massif boasts wide mountain pastures and forests of chestnut. The earth is still fertile. Giacomo Casanova, the 18th-century adventurer, who found the region too austere, wrote, 'The inhabitants loathe work, and their happiness is complete when they find someone willing to take away the fruits which the earth spontaneously and abundantly produces ...'

In fact, for complex social and historical reasons, the people of the *Mezzogiorno* are far less interested in production and trade than their neighbours in the north. The southern aristocracy have always attached more importance to possessing rather than creating wealth. This is due not so much to laziness as to a social system which has prized political influence above all else. As a result of this mentality, the more able southerners have tended to make their careers in politics and government administration. Since the post-war industrial boom in the North, however, millions of peasants from the South have left their lands for the factories of Milan and Turin.

The *Mezzogiorno* offers landscapes of savage and unspoilt beauty. The coast of Basilicata, for instance, is harsh and imposing, with cliffs, promontories and secret inlets. Inland, the Pollino mountain range is an exceptional nature reserve where wolves, wild boar, porcupines, ibex and deer run freely among forests of beech and oak.

Farther east, Puglia has a more gentle aspect. Fields of wheat alternate with pine woods, and the air is full of the scent of jasmine and bergamot. Many of the towns are beautiful, too: places such as Taranto, a naval base with a spectacular natural harbour, excellent fish restaurants, and an archaeological museum filled with treasures from the ancient Greek civilisation that once flourished here. Even more outstanding is Lecce, a baroque gem on Puglia's eastern side. It is the profusion of decorative details on the convents, churches and palaces that makes a stroll through Lecce's streets so memorable. Minutely sculpted carvings festoon the façades of buildings and the fountains plashing in courtyards and squares. Gates and balconies display wonderfully exuberant wrought-iron work. And all is dominated by the softly golden tints of the *pietra di Lecce*, the local sandstone.

Atrani, on the Amalfi coast, its houses artfully stacked into the narrow space between cliffs and sea. The first inhabitants took refuge here from the invading Goths and Lombards.

Puglia also has its own unique form of domestic architecture in the form of *trulli* – beehive-shaped houses with thick walls and domes built of flat stones. They are both spacious and beautifully insulated from heat and cold. The greatest concentration of these structures is in Alberobello, Locorotondo and Martina Franca, in the hinterland between Bari and Brindisi.

Calabria, the southernmost region of mainland Italy, is equally fascinating. Although its coast has been somewhat tastelessly developed, the inland areas are intact – a wilderness of gorges, ravines, thick forests and valleys carpeted with flowers, with strange villages cut off from the world. Some are peopled by Albanians, who arrived in the 15th century and continue to speak Albanian and worship in the Orthodox faith. In other villages the women wear green skirts and white blouses with puffed sleeves that are oddly reminiscent of Switzerland – and with good reason, for they are the descendants of Waldensian heretics who were given refuge here by the Holy Roman Emperor Frederick II in the 13th century. Calabria is full of such surprises, but fortunately few nasty ones. You are unlikely these days to be set upon by bandits, for the notorious *'ndrangheta* (or Calabrian Mafia) have found more lucrative activities than robbing travellers.

The farther down the 'boot' of Italy, the more the Apennines taper, offering views westward to the Tyrrhenian Sea at one place, then south-east to the Ionian in another, until there comes a magical point – at Aspromonte – where you can see both at once. The mountains finally plunge into the sea, giving a definite impression that you have reached *finis terrae*, the end of the earth. Beyond, though, the white ferries crossing the turquoise waters are a reminder that there is still another Italy to explore, the Italy of the islands.

Sicily's two faces

Sicily looks quite different from the southern Italian mainland, despite the many historical links binding the two. Instead of the peaks and gorges of Calabria, Sicily presents a landscape of ample curves: wide valleys, rounded mountains, vast treeless plateaus planted with

Sicilian peasants ride home from the fields. Despite widespread mechanisation, the horse is still popular – a legacy of either the Norman or the Arab occupation.

Sicily is no longer the 'granary of Italy' that it was under the Romans, but agriculture – particularly the cultivation of wheat, citrus fruit, tomatoes and almonds – remains the backbone of its economy.

A house in Palermo. The dilapidated, neglected walls tell their own sad story of the struggle for existence in the underside of Italy's 30-year fairy tale of success.

wheat. Even the domineering bulk of Etna fails to disturb this pattern, its solidified rivers of lava and black ash spreading in soft undulations across hundreds of square miles of fertile land. The people look different, too. Sunburnt, stocky and short-legged, they are solid rather than graceful. They are less expansive than other Italians, less immediately friendly. They will usually watch a stranger come into a village in silence and make no effort to open a conversation. Everything conspires to make you think that you are on a different continent – not quite Africa, but not exactly Europe either.

Fishermen mending nets in Syracuse, near Sicily's south-eastern corner. The city now has only a third of the population it had in 287 BC when the inventor and mathematician Archimedes was born there.

At the junction of two seas, the Ionian and the Tyrrhenian, Sicily's coastal waters are rich in fish, especially tuna and swordfish. Swordfish are particularly common in the Strait of Messina between Sicily and the mainland.

A Sicilian fisherman and his boat. Note the eye painted on the bow, a possible relic from ancient Greek times – the Greeks had eyes painted on their triremes. It also serves as a talisman against the malocchio, *the evil eye.*

This is a false impression, or at best only half-true – first of all, because there have traditionally been two Sicilies, not one. The east, which fell mainly under Greek influence, has a tradition of being democratic, tolerant, urbane and reasonably prosperous. The west, whose principal influences are Norman and Arabic, has tended to be more feudal, violent and poor, and is where the Mafia was born. Palermo is the city of Mafia shootings, with over 100 murders a year. To get a job or a driving licence, or secure any kind of business deal, you have to pass through the hands of the 'honoured society'. The town of Villalba, in the west, is the traditional Mafia capital. If you try mentioning the name of Don Calogero Vizzini, who was mayor here and Mafia 'godfather' until his death in 1954, you will not find anyone willing to pursue the conversation. They do not talk to strangers, and the only foreigners they welcome are their returning sons, back from successful careers in New York and Chicago.

The persistence and power of the Mafia can be explained in part by history. Sicilians have been governed almost continuously by foreigners. Their defence has been to evolve their own parallel social system, operating according to its own laws, based on family and community loyalties. The 'family' in Sicily is an extended family – practically a clan – that includes uncles, aunts, cousins, all the collateral kin, the in-laws with their uncles, aunts and cousins, the godparents, witnesses at family weddings, servants, tenants and employees. It is within this primitive community that disputes are settled and solidarity is felt. The village and the Mafia are extensions of it, serving to resolve the problems which in other countries are regarded as the business of the state. Everything is discussed and

Sicily's reputation as a place of violence and poverty can be misleading. Parts of the island are lush and fertile, and have as strong a claim as anywhere in the Mediterranean to be called a natural paradise.

arranged between people who know each other, either personally or through their families. In this way, society is a complicated network of personal favours between men of all classes.

All this is less true in the east of Sicily, where the Greek influence has never waned. As in ancient Athens, social life has long been more fluid and open. The family is still important, but is much less introverted, less proud, and less bitterly engaged in vendetta. Women are freer, the law more respected, and society more organised. Ancient Greece has left its stamp on the countryside, too: in the temples and theatres that abound from Taormina to Agrigento. Syracuse, the

native city of Archimedes, offers groups of ancient monuments the likes of which you will scarcely find even in Greece, and the Valley of the Temples at Agrigento is one of the great classical sites of the Mediterranean. Everywhere there is evidence of the Greeks' sureness of eye in choosing the position for a town or temple: their buildings seem placed not only to fit into nature but to perfect it.

Sicily has always been part of other people's plans, and never had a chance to forge its own. Invaded by Phoenicians, Greeks, Carthaginians, Romans, Vandals, Ostrogoths, Byzantines, Arabs, Normans, Spaniards and finally northern Italians, the island and its people bear

One of the famous carved and painted carts which, along with the puppet theatre, are the glory of Sicilian folk art.

Oleander grows plentifully all over Italy, from pots on sixth-floor balconies to the central reservations on motorways.

many traces of their passage, and have done little for themselves culturally, except to combine foreign influences – Greco-Roman, Arabo-Norman, Angevin-Spanish, and so on. Not that these combinations are without charm: there are wonderfully outlandish churches with massive Norman walls, delicate Gothic windows and doors, and red or blue domes that could only have come from Africa. The 13th-century cathedral of Monreale, 5 miles south-west of Palermo, is a particularly successful example, with its Moorish cloisters, Arabo-Norman walls and Byzantine mosaics.

In the final analysis, though, Sicily remains an Italian island. It is true that the Sicilians do not smile much, that they make little effort to please strangers and foreigners, but once you have established contact with them, you find lively, quick-witted, expressive people who do all the classic Italian things.

The journalist Luigi Barzini remarked that Sicily is like a shaving-mirror to the rest of Italy: it shows up, in magnified form, all the defects as well as the qualities of the Italians. A number of Italy's greatest writers – Pirandello, Sciascia, Tomasi di Lampedusa, Vittorini – have been Sicilians, and Italian culture this century would unquestionably be poorer without them.

Traditional costume in the Sardinian village of Sinnai displays the wealth of local craftsmanship, which includes work in gold, silver, iron, leather, coral, basketry, lace and weaving.

Italian bread is much lighter than its English counterpart. Rolls are generally preferred to loaves in the North, although good bakeries also sell pane pugliese *and* pane toscano, *both of which come in big roundels like millstones.*

Fish traps being made in Bosa, on the west coast of Sardinia. Fishing is not a major activity in Sardinia, and the few fishermen continue to use traditional methods, including the trident.

Sardinia: island outpost

Sardinia is far harder to fit into the Italian matrix. Although the island has known the same invaders, they never stayed long, and left fewer traces. The only ruins of any importance are the *nuraghi,* conical fortress-houses which predate even the Romans. Despite their island's position as a maritime crossroads between Spain, Italy, France and Africa, Sardinians have remained doggedly themselves, taking little from the outside world and giving back even less.

They are a closed, silent, determined people, with none of the easy charm, urban civilisation or artistic talents of mainland Italians. Their virtues are those of the countryman: hospitality, obstinacy, frugality and gravity. Rome, Florence and Naples seem light years away. The Sardinians, as the British writer D.H. Lawrence pointed out, are in fact much closer to the Celtic peoples of Brittany and Ireland. And like the Celts they are proudly separatist – an autonomous region within the Italian republic, with their own language, Sardo. There are some anomalies, however. Half the inhabitants of the west-coast town of Alghero speak Catalan (a relic of the time in the Middle Ages when they were part of Barcelona's maritime empire), and half speak Sardo – with the result that signposts and the like have to be in Italian for both sides to understand.

The countryside has a Celtic feel, too. There is none of that sense of artistic placing and shaping that you find in northern Italy or eastern Sicily. Here nature is free, majestic and wild. From the rocky islets of the north to the high cliffs of the south, Sardinia offers a splendid succession of landscapes, from prairies to forests and mountains. The island is thinly populated (1 million people in 9300 square miles), with most of the inhabitants concentrated in the cities of Cagliari and Sassari, leaving vast rural areas to shepherds and their sheep. Local festivals abound, with one of the most spectacular at Mamoiada in the centre of the island: the festivities involve ritual dances by men wearing masks and sheepskins, and the slaughtering of a 'scapegoat'.

In the quiet solitudes of Sardinia you have a sense – rare in Italy – of exploration and discovery. You may also feel the odd frisson of fear, for these desolate places have for centuries been the home of Sardinian bandits. As you drive up to Orgosolo, the landscape becomes harsher, the road narrower and more deserted, until finally you reach the town, which is a series of unfinished buildings inhabited by old men and tragic women waiting endlessly for their sons and husbands to return from their voyages overseas.

If the harshness of Sardinia becomes too much for you, and you feel the need to make contact with the refinement and verve of Italy again, you need only go as far as Carloforte, a charming little island off the southern tip of Sardinia, where both the food and the dialect are Genoese. The inhabitants of this curious place are Ligurians and Piedmontese who came here three centuries ago, having colonised Tabarka in Tunisia, where they picked up a taste for *couscous* without losing any of their native traditions. This, at last, is Italy again, in all its glorious unpredictability.

Tomatoes hanging out to dry in the Lipari (or Aeolian) Islands, off the north-east coast of Sicily.

Gazetteer

Spain

The Iberian peninsula (present-day Spain and Portugal) was occupied by men of Stone Age culture as long ago as 13,000 BC. They developed a strong pictorial art, evidence of which can be seen in the cave-paintings of north-west Spain. The Iberians entered Spain from Africa in c. 3000 BC and they mingled with Celtic tribes from the north during the 4th century to form the so-called Celtiberian culture. Between 1100 BC and 509 BC the peninsula was invaded in turn by Phoenicians, Greeks and Carthaginians who were all interested in the country's rich mineral resources of silver, iron and copper.

The Romans expelled the Carthaginians from the peninsula and began to subdue the independent Iberian tribes. They made Spain a single political unit, linking its regions together by roads, and the peninsula became known as Hispania.

The Visigoths, one of the Germanic tribes who invaded the Roman Empire, conquered most of the peninsula in AD 475. They were unable to establish stable political rule or to assimilate the subject Hispano-Romans, although in time they adopted Christianity from them.

The expansion of the militant new faith of Islam had a profound impact on Spanish history. In 711 and 712, Arab and Berber armies crossed the Strait of Gibraltar from Africa and within eight years the invaders had conquered the entire peninsula, except the mountainous regions of the north where Christianity prevailed. For the next six centuries, Spain remained divided between Christians and Moors, as the Muslim invaders were known.

The power of the Moors declined following the break-up of the Caliphate of Cordoba in 1002; slowly the Christian forces pushed them south until by the end of the 13th century only Granada remained under Moorish control. The Christian reconquest was not a continuous process. In the 13th century, under Castilian leadership, it became a religious crusade; strict Catholic orthodoxy and racial purity became the hallmarks of a new Spanish nationalism. This led to the foundation of the Spanish Inquisition, a court controlled by the Spanish kings, whose purpose was to root out heresy. The Jews were expelled from Spain fourteen years later, in 1492.

In the same year, the Italian Christopher Columbus, sailing under the Spanish flag, discovered the New World. The foundations of Spanish power in Europe and the Americas were laid.

The years of the Habsburg dynasty saw the rise and decline of Spain as a great power. In 1516 Charles I, the first of the Habsburg line in Spain, was crowned. He was later elected

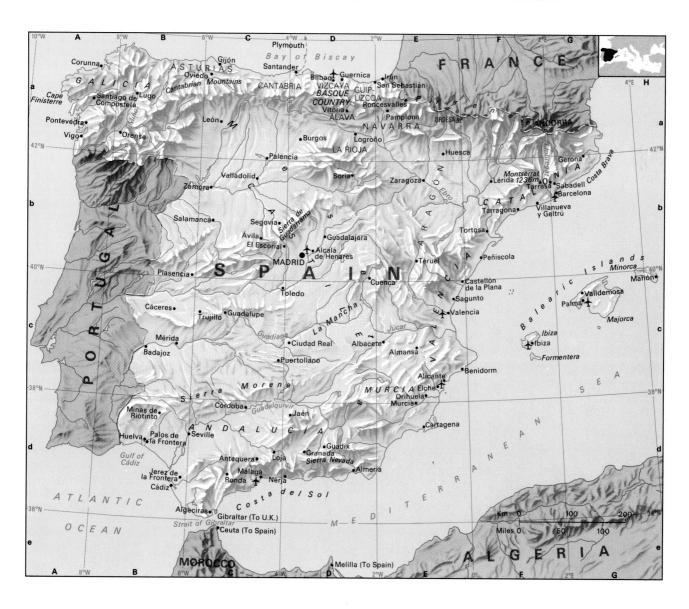

SPAIN AT A GLANCE

Area 194,897 square miles	
Population 38,820,000	
Capital Madrid	
Government Parliamentary monarchy	
Currency Peseta = 100 centimos	
Languages Castilian Spanish (official), Catalan, Galician, Basque	
Religion Christian (predominantly Roman Catholic; about 90,000 Protestants)	
Climate Mediterranean in the southern and eastern coastlands, temperate elsewhere. Average temperature in Madrid ranges from 1-8°C (34-46°F) in January to 17-31°C (63-88°F) in July	
Main primary products Cereals, fruit, vegetables, sugar cane, grapes, tobacco, cotton, almonds, olives, timber, cork, fish; coal, lignite, iron, lead, copper, tin, zinc, mercury, tungsten	
Major industries Agriculture, food processing, wine making, yarns, textiles, iron and steel, mining, petroleum refining, chemicals, engineering, transport equipment, forestry and timber products, fishing, cement manufacture, metal processing	
Main exports Machinery, motor vehicles, fruit and vegetables, wine, olive oil, iron and steel, chemicals, petroleum products, small metal manufactures, shoes, textiles	
Annual income per head (US$) 10,100	
Population growth (per thous/yr) 5	
Life expectancy (yrs) Male 72 Female 76	

Holy Roman Emperor, taking the title Charles V. His interests remained largely in Germany, and the rich rewards of silver and gold from Spanish conquests of Mexico and Peru paid for Charles's interests outside Spain. He ended his reign bankrupt.

Under Charles's son, Philip II, Spain became the greatest power in Europe. With the annexation of Portugal in 1580, the entire Iberian peninsula came under Spanish rule. However, Spain's economy was collapsing. Philip saw Spain as the sole defender of Catholicism in Europe. He fought against the Protestant Netherlands and England. But in 1581, after years of conflict, the Netherlands broke free to form the Dutch Republic and this, together with the defeat of the Spanish Armada in 1588, led to the decline of Spain as the dominant European power.

Under Philip's weak successors, Spain sank deeper into decline. Prolonged wars with its chief rival, France, bled Spain's resources dry; Portugal was lost and Catalonia revolted.

The last of the Spanish Habsburgs, Charles II, died heirless in 1700. After a decade of the War of the Spanish Succession the Bourbon prince Philip of Anjou became King of Spain. The 18th century saw a remarkable Spanish recovery. The Bourbons encouraged industry, built roads and improved the administration of Spain's American empire.

In 1808, Napoleon Bonaparte marched into Spain and made his brother king. The Bourbon king, Ferdinand VIII, was held captive in France. Ferdinand returned to the throne in 1814 after the French were driven from Spain in the Peninsular War.

Between 1814 and 1874 there was great rivalry between the liberals and the conservatives. On Ferdinand's death in 1833, the liberals wanted the monarchy to go to his three-year-old daughter, Isabella, while the conservatives favoured Ferdinand's brother, Don Carlos, a devout Catholic. The movement supporting Don Carlos became known as Carlism and disrupted Spain for the next fifty years. In 1833 there was civil war between the Carlists and the liberals. Isabella's supporters won, but the rest of her reign was a confused struggle between the forces of constitutional government and despotism. In 1863 a revolution dethroned Isabella and the First Republic was established in 1873. A year later another revolution brought Isabella's son, Alfonso, to the throne.

Under Alfonso XII, it became customary for liberals and conservatives to hold office in turn, but this apparently democratic system was marked by extensive corruption behind the scenes. The period was also one of economic growth at home, although abroad Spain lost Cuba, Puerto Rico and the Philippines – almost all of its remaining empire.

The first two decades of the 20th century under Alfonso XIII were years of acute unrest in Spain; Catalonia, a region with its own separate culture and prosperous economy, pressed for political independence and there were bitter clashes in Catalonia's chief city, Barcelona, between employers and the Confederacion Nacional del Trabajo, an anarchic trade union, which believed that the state was an instrument of oppression and should be destroyed.

In 1923, Miguel Primo de Riviera, Captain-General of Catalonia, set up a dictatorship backed by Alfonso. At first he was popular, but when Spain's prosperity diminished with the fall of the peseta in 1929, he was forced to resign.

In 1931, the first freely held municipal elections for eight years led to victory for the republican parties and the Second Republic was declared. At first the liberals held leadership but in 1936 they fell to a 'Popular Front'. Simultaneously, however, General Francisco Franco who had been semi-exiled by the Republican government, took command of Spanish forces in Morocco and led them in an invasion of Spain.

Spain quickly split into two armed camps – the army supporters or Nationalists, and the government supporters or Loyalists. General Franco soon emerged as an unchallenged leader of the Nationalists and they were eventually victorious as their troops entered Madrid in 1939.

The new Spanish state under Franco was harshly authoritarian, based on the support of the Falange – the Spanish Fascist party – the army, and the Catholic Church. Spain remained neutral in the Second World War, but despite Allied victory was an outcast among European nations until 1955 when it was admitted to the United Nations.

In 1972, Franco appointed Prince Juan Carlos, grandson of Alfonso XIII, eventually to succeed him as chief of state, and following Franco's death in 1974 he became King Juan Carlos I. The king initiated a movement towards a more democratic Spain. In June 1977 he held the first free election since the Civil War to elect a new parliament, and a new constitution approved by national referendum came into effect at the end of 1978.

Although recession slowed industrial growth in the early 1980s, Spain has greatly diversified its economy in recent decades. Tourism has become an important industry with some 40 million tourists visiting Spain each year. Military and economic isolation ended with Spain joining the NATO alliance in 1982 and entering the European Community in 1986.

These changes brought economic growth to Spain and it entered the 1990s with the peseta as one of the strongest currencies in the EC Exchange Rate Mechanism.

Portugal

Cut off by Spain from direct contact with the rest of Europe, the Portuguese have for centuries looked outwards to land overseas. Their sailors founded an empire in the 15th century in lands as far apart as Africa, Brazil and India.

The original people of the Iberian peninsula – which is made up of Portugal and Spain – were subdued by the Carthaginians in the 6th century BC, who were in turn defeated by the Romans in 206 BC. They divided the peninsula into three provinces, the most western of which, Lusitania, corresponded roughly to modern Portugal. As the Roman Empire disintegrated in the 5th century AD, the peninsula was overrun by Visigoths and other northern barbarians. Three centuries later, the Visigoths were defeated by the Moorish rulers of the Islamic Empire in North Africa.

By the 12th century, the Moors were being driven south by a Christian reconquest from Spain. One of the volunteers, Henry of Burgundy, was rewarded for his service to King Alfonso VI of Castile with the hand of the king's illegitimate daughter and the 'county' of Portugal (the northern third of the present state).

Henry's son, Afonso Henriques, threw off the yoke of Castile and in 1143 was recognised as king of an independent Portugal. Portugal's early kings pushed their southern frontier ever deeper into Moorish territory and by 1279 the boundaries of Portugal as they are today were accomplished.

One of the most outstanding medieval kings of Portugal was Diniz who reigned from 1279 until 1325. He was responsible for encouraging foreign trade by establishing a commercial treaty with England, and he started a navy, thus laying the foundation for Portugal's future greatness.

The impetus generated by Diniz was not maintained by his successors who for the next 60 years were frequently involved in wars and disputes with Castile and with the Moors. In May 1386, the Treaty of Windsor marked the formal alliance of Portugal and England and was cemented in 1387 by the marriage of John I of Portugal to the daughter of John of Gaunt, a powerful English noble.

The son born of this marriage, Henry the Navigator (1394-1460), initiated the most splendid era of Portuguese history, being the patron and inspirer of Portugal's first voyages of exploration. Henry's captains went on to discover Madeira, the Azores, Senegal and the Cape Verde Islands.

The voyages did not cease with Henry's death; Bartholomew Diaz rounded the southernmost tip of Africa in 1488; Vasco da Gama reached India in 1498. Within a few years the Portuguese had staked out a world-wide empire. This 'golden

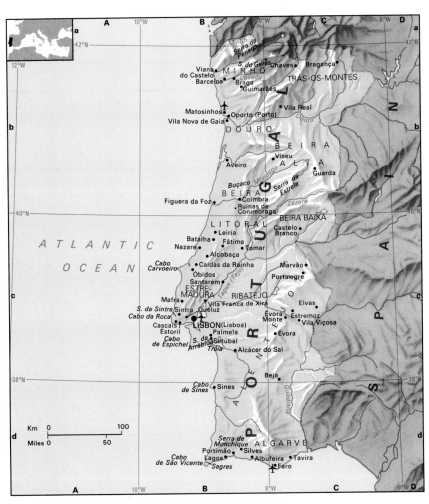

PORTUGAL AT A GLANCE
Area 35,553 square miles
Population 10,000,000
Capital Lisbon
Government Parliamentary republic
Currency Escudo = 100 centavos
Language Portuguese
Religion Christian (96% Roman Catholic)
Climate Hot dry summers, warm moist winters; average temperature in Lisbon ranges from 8-14°C (46-57°F) in January to 17-28°C (63-82°F) in August
Main primary products Cereals, olives, timber, rice, grapes, citrus fruits and vegetables, cork, fish; copper, salt, iron, tungsten, tin
Major industries Agriculture, textiles, machinery, food processing, wood products, chemicals, wine, fishing, mining, tourism
Main exports Textiles, machinery, petroleum products, chemicals, cork, wine, sardines
Annual income per head (US$) 6900
Population growth (per thous/yr) 5
Life expectancy (yrs) Male 70 Female 75

age' of Portugal was achieved under Manuel I (1495-1521).

Manuel's son, John III, fell increasingly under the influence of his religious advisers. When he died, leaving the throne to his three-year-old son, the Jesuits ran the country as regents. When Sebastian came of age he embarked on a 'crusade' into Morocco which ended in his death in 1578. Prince Henry, Sebastian's great-uncle, inherited the throne but died within 18 months.

There were several claimants to the vacant throne but Philip II of Spain, the nephew of John III, was installed by force of arms and the backing of the Jesuits. For the next 60 years Portugal remained under Spain's dominance. In 1640 a bloodless coup restored independence, but Spain did not release Portugal without a struggle and intermittent war between the two countries lasted for 28 years.

Though the glories of the Portuguese Empire were much diminished, the discovery of gold and diamond fields in Brazil in 1693 brought a vast flow of revenue to the Braganza kings, enabling them to rule as absolute monarchs until the mid-18th century. One far-sighted statesman, the Marquis of Pombal, saw the danger of reliance on one source of revenue from the other side of the Atlantic. From 1755 until King Joseph's death in 1777, he was the effective ruler of Portugal introducing reforms in finance, industry, education and the armed forces. These reforms were brought to an end when Pombal was dismissed by Joseph's successor, the unbalanced Maria I.

When the Napoleonic Wars broke out, France invaded, capturing Lisbon in 1807. British troops were sent to Portugal and, along with Portuguese regiments, drove the French out.

Portugal shared in the general radical ferment which convulsed Europe in the 19th century; strikes, peasant risings and army mutinies ushered in the 20th century, and in 1910 a republic was proclaimed.

In 1926, General Carmona seized power and two years later he appointed Dr Salazar as his finance minister. Salazar balanced the budget and became premier in 1932. He ruled for the next 36 years, giving the country much-needed stability.

In 1983 the Socialists gained power in national elections; they introduced stringent austerity measures to beat inflation and in 1986 joined the European Community. But Portugal remained one of the poorest countries in Western Europe and, as the 1990s began, massive amounts of EC aid started pouring in to help turn Portugal into a modern industrial state.

Yugoslavia

The people of this rugged, mountainous country achieved nationhood after the First World War, when Serbia, Montenegro, Croatia, Slovenia, Bosnia-Herzegovina and Macedonia were united to form the kingdom of Yugoslavia – the 'land of the South Slavs'.

The territory which makes up Yugoslavia was once part of the Roman Empire. Following the withdrawal of the Romans the region came under the influence of Byzantium, but in the 7th century AD they were driven into the mountains by Slav invaders from the east.

By the 14th century the Slav state of Serbia was the dominant Balkan power, having conquered Macedonia and parts of Greece. Its greatest ruler, Stephen Dushan, planned to attack the Byzantine Empire, but he died on his march to Constantinople in 1355. Serbia later disintegrated under attack by the Ottoman Turks, who finally conquered the country in 1459.

From the mid-15th to the mid-19th centuries most of Yugoslavia was part of the Ottoman Empire. In 1878 the Congress of Berlin freed Serbia and Montenegro. But Turkey kept its hold on Macedonia, while Austria-Hungary annexed Bosnia-Herzegovina in 1908.

YUGOSLAVIA AT A GLANCE
BOSNIA-HERZEGOVINA
Area 19,736 square miles
Population 4,440,000
Capital Sarajevo

CROATIA
Area 21,824 square miles
Population 4,680,000
Capital Zagreb

MACEDONIA
Area 9928 square miles
Population 2,090,000
Capital Skopje

MONTENEGRO
Area 5331 square miles
Population 632,000
Capital Titograd

SERBIA
Area 34,107 square miles
Population 9,760,000
Capital Belgrade

SLOVENIA
Area 7817 square miles
Population 1,940,000
Capital Ljubljana

In June 1914, Gavrilo Princip, who belonged to a
Serbian nationalist society known as the 'Black Hand',
assassinated Archduke Franz Ferdinand, heir to the Austro-
Hungarian throne, at Sarajevo. Austria-Hungary declared war
on Serbia; Russia, Germany and the other great European
powers were drawn in and the First World War had begun.
The surrender of Germany, Austria and Turkey in 1918 was
followed by the creation of Yugoslavia under the rule of Peter I
of Serbia.

The newly united Slavs soon quarrelled among themselves.
Rivalry between the Croats and the Serbs for political
supremacy led Alexander I to set up a royal dictatorship in
1929, but he was assassinated in 1934. In the 1930s the
disunited country came increasingly under the influence of the
Axis powers, Germany and Italy. Finally the regent, Paul,
joined the Axis in 1941, but he was overthrown by a popular
uprising. Germany immediately invaded the country.

Resistance movements sprang up to fight the Germans. But
many Croats supported the occupying forces, while some
supporters of the royalist Chetniks led by a Serb general,
Draga Mihajlovic, fought against Tito's Communist partisans.
By 1944 Tito (born Josip Broz) had emerged as victor against
Mihajlovic (who was later executed) and in 1945 he assumed
the leadership of the liberated country and abolished the
monarchy.

The Soviet leaders expected Tito's Yugoslavia to be an
obedient puppet state, but in 1948 Tito refused to toe the
Stalinist line and Yugoslavia was expelled from the Soviet bloc.
After Stalin's death in 1953, the new Soviet leaders
re-established friendly relations, but Tito still resisted any
attempt to make him follow the Kremlin's dictates and he
accepted aid from both East and West to bring prosperity to his
people.

The last survivor of the Second World War's major figures,
Tito, at 87, still held firm political control when he died in
1980. Milka Planinc was elected prime minister by parliament
in 1982 – the first woman to head the government. Under
Planinc, Yugoslavia maintained its policy of non-alignment
throughout the 1980s. But without Tito's charismatic presence
to hold the jealous nationalities together, the country slowly
began to fragment.

Slovenia and Croatia declared their independence in 1991,
which led to conflict with the Serbian-dominated Federal
Army. In 1992, the European Community recognised the two
new states, but EC sanctions against Serbia did not stop the
fighting as Bosnia-Herzegovina struggled for its own
independence.

Both the United Nations and the European Community
tried to act as peace brokers in the conflict, but their efforts
were largely unsuccessful. In June 1992 the United Nations
imposed sanctions against Serbia, which included an oil
embargo and a total ban on trade.

GREECE AT A GLANCE

Area 50,960 square miles
Population 10,000,000
Capital Athens
Government Parliamentary republic
Currency Drachma = 100 lepta
Language Greek
Religions Christian (98% Greek Orthodox), Muslim (1%)
Climate Mediterranean; average temperature in Athens ranges from 6-13°C (43-55°F) in February to 23-33°C (73-91°F) in July
Main primary products Wheat, tobacco, cotton, sugar beet, olives, grapes, fruit, vegetables; iron, bauxite, nickel, zinc, lead, lignite, chrome, marble, magnesite, barytes, salt, crude oil
Major industries Agriculture, textiles, cement, fertilisers, steel, chemicals, tobacco products, food processing, aluminium smelting, consumer products, wine, shipbuilding, tourism
Main exports Fruit and vegetables, petroleum products, textiles, clothing, iron and steel, tobacco, cement, aluminium, chemicals, metal ores
Annual income per head (US$) 5605
Population growth (per thous/yr) 6
Life expectancy (yrs) Male 71 Female 75

Greece

Despite the spread of classical Greek civilisation beyond its
regional boundaries, there was never a Greek 'empire' like the
Roman Empire. The only thing the Hellenes (Greeks) had in
common was their language and culture and, apart from that,
they fought bitterly.

The earliest known civilisation in Greece was the non-
Greek Minoan culture of Crete, which developed c. 3000 BC.
Crete became the centre of a Maritime empire until c. 1400
when this collapsed and Mycenaean Greeks, the first Greek-
speaking people, took over. The Mycenaean culture collapsed
in about 1200 BC when the Dorians, another Greek-speaking
civilisation from the north, invaded.

The next culture to emerge was that of the Athenians, who
successfully defended Greece's Ionian colonies from numerous
invasions by Persia between 450 and 479 BC. However, such
dominance stirred Corinth and other states to combine against
Athens under the leadership of Sparta in the Peloponnesian War
(431-404 BC), and Athenian dominance was destroyed for ever.

In 338 BC, Philip of Macedon won a victory at Chaeronea which made him master of Greece. Soon afterwards he was assassinated and his son, Alexander, was left to realise Philip's dream of conquest in Asia. In little more than a decade he successfully invaded the East, from Egypt to the threshold of India. Thus the Hellenic culture spread.

Following their surrender to Philip, the Greeks were destined to remain a subject people for more than 2000 years. Roman legions broke Macedonian dominance in 168 BC and in 146 BC Greece became a Roman province. When the Roman Empire was divided in AD 330, Greece fell into the eastern or Byzantine half and so continued with no separate history or identity until the Turks conquered Constantinople in 1453.

The fall of Constantinople led to the splitting of the Greek peninsula into a number of feudal domains, and for about four centuries Greece stagnated as a province of the Ottoman Empire.

From 1814 onwards a growing nationalist movement against the Turks developed and, in 1821, there was an armed uprising which was answered with savage repression. The combined fleets of Britain, France and Russia intervened and destroyed the Turkish and Egyptian fleets at Navarino in 1827. By 1832 Greece was fully independent. Their first president was assassinated and it was decided that Greece should become a monarchy.

In the First World War the Greeks were neutral at first, but they joined the Allies against Turkey. They gained Thrace at the peace conference, but still dissatisfied, launched their own war against Turkey in 1921. They were totally defeated. A republic was proclaimed in 1924, but in 1935 the monarchy was restored by an overwhelming popular vote. Parliamentary democracy produced no stability and a fascist-style dictatorship was established in 1936.

In 1940 Mussolini, the Italian dictator, invaded Greece and would have been defeated had it not been for the intervention of Italy's ally, Germany, who subsequently occupied Greece until 1944, when the country was liberated by British troops. Civil war broke out in 1946 between the Communist-led guerrilla groups, who had been fighting the Germans, and the monarchist government. It was not until 1950 that the government won.

In 1967 a coup brought a military junta into power. Colonel George Papadopoulos was named as premier and defence minister. King Constantine XIII attempted a counter-coup, failed and went into exile. In 1973 Papadopoulos established a republic with himself as president, but within months he was deposed by another military junta. A confrontation between Greece and Turkey, triggered by the overthrow of the Cyprus government, resulted in the collapse of the new junta in 1974.

Constantine Karamanlis, a conservative, was sworn in as the new premier and returned the nation to parliamentary democracy. He turned the leadership of his party over to younger men in 1980 and became president until 1985. The Socialist party took over in 1981; and in the same year Greece became a member of the EEC but did not gain any immediate benefit from the expanded trade opportunities.

Italy

ITALY AT A GLANCE
Area 116,304 square miles
Population 57,320,000
Capital Rome
Government Parliamentary republic
Currency Lira = 100 centesimi
Languages Italian, some French, German and Slovene
Religion Christian (83% Roman Catholic)
Climate Mediterranean; average temperature in Rome ranges from 4-11°C (39-52°F) in January to 20-30°C (68-86°F) in July
Main primary products Cereals, potatoes, sugar, vegetables, soft fruits, citrus fruits, grapes, olives, livestock, fish; oil and natural gas, asbestos, potash, iron ore, zinc, mercury, sulphur, marble
Major industries Iron and steel, motor vehicles, chemicals, oil and gas refining, machinery, textiles, clothing, agriculture, food processing, wine, fishing, tourism
Main exports Machinery, chemicals, petroleum products, motor vehicles, clothing, food, textile yarns and fabrics, iron and steel, footwear
Annual income per head (US$) 14,000
Population growth (per thous/yr) 3
Life expectancy (yrs) Male 72 Female 76

The people of the Italian peninsula achieved nationhood only in the 1860s. The strongly regional character of the country has always made for disunity, as well as giving Italian life and history their great richness and variety.

About 3000 years ago, the mountainous Italian peninsula was thickly forested and dotted with tribal settlements, whose people were of a primitive Bronze Age culture. Cities emerged with the arrival of more civilised colonists.

The Greeks established ports in Sicily and the south of Italy as far north as Naples. In central Italy there flourished the civilisation of the Etruscans, a people of uncertain origins who were greatly skilled in architecture and engineering. Rome began as an insignificant settlement of one of the native Latin tribes. Its petty kings were Etruscans.

The Romans drove out the last of their Etruscan kings, Tarquinius Superbus, in 509 BC. In place of the monarchy they set up a republic, though this was split by class conflict between patricians (aristocrats) and plebeians (commoners). Nevertheless, the Romans gradually imposed a unified government on the entire peninsula. They then proceeded to expand their power, until their boundaries extended to the English Channel, the Rhine and the Danube. In the east, they ruled Egypt, Syria and much of Asia Minor.

In the 4th century AD Christian Rome's distant frontiers crumbled under the pressure of nomadic barbarian tribes. The country fragmented under the blows of the invaders.

Meanwhile Byzantium, the eastern half of the Roman Empire with its capital at Constantinople, temporarily liberated much of Italy from the barbarians. The Byzantines held Sicily, Rome, Ravenna, Naples and other scattered areas, between which stretched the great northern kingdom of the duchies of Spoleto and Benevento which were ruled by another barbarian tribe, the Lombards. In this dark age of anarchy, a group of Italians founded Venice as a refuge among lagoons.

In Rome, the citizens, lacking a leader, turned to their bishop, Pope Gregory the Great, and so gave the papacy its status as a political power. Later popes appealed to Pepin, King of the Franks, and his successor, Charlemagne, to march into Italy and subdue the Lombards. On Christmas Day, 800, in the Church of St Peter in Rome, Pope Leo III crowned Charlemagne Holy Roman Emperor, in succession to the Caesars. But this did not restore the peace and unity which the Italians had enjoyed under the old Roman Empire.

Throughout the Middle Ages, Italy was split into many different states, large and small. The papacy was the only force for unity, but the political influence of the popes fluctuated. After the election of the Frenchman Clement V in 1305, a succession of French popes kept their court at Avignon for 70 years. Pope Gregory XI attempted to return to Rome, but a further controversy shortly after his death in 1378 led to the 'Great Schism'. For the next 40 years the Catholic Church had two rival popes, one with his palace in Avignon and the other in Rome, each supported by a bloc of foreign powers. Only after 1417 was the division healed. The papacy was re-established in Rome and the city became once more a main centre of Italian life.

During the 14th century Florence, Milan and Venice gained steadily in power. On the basis of their economic strength, these three Italian cities built up a financial and military supremacy. Other cities became their satellites.

Naples and Sicily in the south remained feudal and backward. Two queens, Joanna I and Joanna II, led scandalous lives but, despite various marriages, both of them failed to provide legitimate heirs. After Joanna II's death in 1435, the south was torn by bloody dynastic struggles between the rival claimants to the throne. The issue was finally settled in 1442 by the triumph of Alfonso of Aragon, known as 'the Magnanimous'.

Though the Italian states maintained an uneasy balance among themselves, they could not merge their interests and find national unity. This left them prey to the ambitions of foreign powers. In 1494 Charles VIII of France invaded Italy, supposedly in support of his claim to the crown of Naples, but in reality because the country was rich and weak.

For the next 65 years, the political framework of Renaissance Italy was shattered by the clash of rival foreign armies. France's attack on Italy soon turned into a struggle with the Holy Roman Emperor for European supremacy. In 1559 the Treaty of Cateau-Cambresis established Habsburg Spain as the dominant power in Italy.

The 18th-century wars of the Spanish and the Austrian succession changed little except the flags under which the Italians lived. By the time of Napoleon, the Austrians had replaced the Spanish in the north. The south was no longer a Spanish province, but a Neapolitan kingdom, ruled by a junior branch of the Spanish Bourbon dynasty, while the border state of Piedmont was united with the island of Sardinia under the ancient House of Savoy.

Napoleon conquered Italy, and tried to impose order on the country, introducing many of the reforms in law and administration that the Revolution had brought to France. But after his fall in 1815 Italy was returned, still disunited, to its reactionary rulers.

The Napoleonic episode, though a failure, had awoken Italian patriotism from its age-old sleep. The Risorgimento ('revival') was led by three strongly contrasted men: Mazzini, an intellectual idealist, Cavour, an eminently practical politician, and Garibaldi, a daring soldier.

Revolutions in 1848 and 1849 failed to expel the Austrians from Italy. Mazzini and Garibaldi then turned to Cavour, now prime minister of Piedmont, who realised that Italian unity could not be achieved without outside intervention. To bring this about he made an alliance with Napoleon III of France. In 1859 Napoleon sent his army against the Austrians in Italy. After their defeats at Magenta and Solferino, the Austrians agreed to withdraw from Lombardy. In the meantime, Garibaldi had conquered Sicily and Naples – the 'Kingdom of the Two Sicilies', ruled by the reactionary Francis II.

Nearly all of Italy, with the exception of Venice and the Papal States, was now united under Piedmontese rule. In 1866, Venice became Italian after the Austrians were again defeated. In 1870 Prussia's attack on France forced Napoleon to withdraw his troops from the Papal States which they had occupied to protect the pope since 1849. This allowed the Italians to occupy Rome, which in 1871 became the capital of united Italy.

Italy made a Triple Alliance with Germany and Austria in 1882. But after the outbreak of the First World War, Italy stayed neutral until May 1915, when it denounced the Alliance and entered the war on the side of France, Russia and Britain – largely as the result of Allied promises of vast territorial gains at the end of the war.

During the confused months after the war, when disillusioned troops were returning home to face poverty and unemployment, a renegade Socialist, Benito Mussolini, launched his anti-Communist movement, the Fascist Party. Mussolini ordered his followers to march on Rome in 1922; the king gave way before this show of force and called on Mussolini to form a government.

Mussolini gradually transformed Italy into a dictatorship. He took the title of 'Il Duce' (the leader) and suppressed parliament, retaining the monarchy as a figurehead.

Despite being linked with Nazi Germany and Japan in an alliance known as the Axis, Italy again remained neutral in 1939. Only in 1940, after the British evacuation at Dunkirk, and when the fall of France was imminent, did Mussolini enter the war. He was sure that Hitler would win and was afraid that the war would end without Italy sharing in the possible spoils.

The Allies captured Sicily in 1943. More and more Italians now saw that Mussolini had led them into disaster. The king, Victor Emmanuel III, had Mussolini arrested and a new Italian government was set up which negotiated an armistice with the Allies. In October 1943, Italy declared war on Germany.

But most of the country was still held by German forces, and Mussolini had been rescued by German paratroops and set up as a Nazi puppet-ruler in northern Italy. The last phase of the Mediterranean war involved a slow, dogged advance by the Allies up the Italian peninsula. In the final days of the war, Mussolini was captured and shot near Como on April 28, 1945.

In 1945, Italy returned to its parliamentary system, but since the king was considered to have been too deeply involved with the Fascists, a republic was set up after a referendum.

The Christian Democrats formed the strongest single party, but they found it impossible, in later elections, to win an overall majority. In recent years, a succession of coalition governments has led to much unrest. In 1983 Bettino Craxi became Italy's first socialist prime minister, heading a five-party coalition.

Despite the political instability, economic growth continued through the 1980s and Italy entered the 1990s as one of the seven richest nations in the world.

Picture Credits

p.9 C. Lénars; p.10 J.Guillard-Scope; bottom Koch-Rapho; p.11 J.Guillard-Scope; p.12 Roy-Explorer; p.13 Charles-Rapho; p.14 top Sarramon-Rapho; bottom Danot-Vandystadt; p.15 R.McLeod; p.16 Claquin-Explorer; p.17 J.Guillard-Scope; p.18 Ducasse-Rapho; p.19 top Ducasse-Rapho; bottom J.Guillard-Scope; p.20 Mayer-Magnum; p.21 Lentini-Ana; p.22 Reichel-Top; p.23 top Reichel-Top; bottom Sioen-Cedri; p.24 Quéméré-Cedri; p.25 left Gleizes-Explorer; right Reichel-Top; p.26 Roy-Explorer; p.27 Hersant-Fotogram; p.28 Quéméré-Cedri; p.29 Sappa-Cedri; p.30 Le Querrec-Magnum; p.31 Silvester-Rapho; p.32 top Tetrel-Explorer; bottom Silvester-Rapho; p.33 Mayer-Magnum; p.34 left Lanceau-Explorer; right Le Querrec-Magnum; p.35 Marmounier-Cedri; p.36 Mayer-Magnum; p.37 left Mayer-Magnum; right Valat-Top; p. 38 Silvester-Rapho; p.39 top C.Lénars; bottom Donnezan-Rapho; p.40 top Stoen-Cedri; bottom Roy-Explorer; p.41 Donnezan-Rapho; p.42 Guillou-Atlas-Photo; p.43 Valos-Gamma; p.44 Picou-Fotogram; p.45 left Vogel-Top; right Vogel-Rapho; p.46 Marmounier-Cedri; p.47 top Vogel-Top; bottom Haines-Rapho; p.48 Harvey-Comos; p.49 Reichel-Top; p.50 top Sappa-Cedri; bottom Berry-Magnum; p.51 Braga-Rapho; p.52 Bonnecarrère-Cedri; p.53 left Marmounier-Cedri; right Gibet-Pix; p.54 Le Querrec-Magnum; p.55 Charles-Rapho; p.56 top Roy-Explorer; bottom Braga-Rapho; p.57 Marmounier-Cedri; p.58 M.Granger; p.59 M.Granger; p.60 Sappa-Cedri; p.61 top J.Bottin; bottom Régior-Explorer; p.62 top Sappa-Cedri; bottom Gaumy-Magnum; p.63 Barbey-Magnum; p.64 Lamontagne-Diaf; p.64/5 Y.Busson; p.65 J.Guillard-Scope; p.66 Barbey-Magnum; p.67 Y.Busson; p.68 Barbey-Magnum; p.69 Sappa-C.E.D.R.I.; p.70 Sappa-C.E.D.R.I.; p.71 Loirat-Explorer; p.72 top Loirat-Explorer;

bottom Loirat-Explorer; p.73 Sappa-C.E.D.R.I.; p.74 M.Guillard-Scope; p.75 Sappa-C.E.D.R.I.; p.76 Cochet-Explorer; p.77 G. de Laubier; p.78 M.Guillard-Scope; p.78/9 Sappa-C.E.D.R.I.; p.79 Sappa-C.E.D.R.I.; p.80 Sappa-C.E.D.R.I.; p.81 top Sappa-C.E.D.R.I.; bottom G. de Laubier; p.82 M.Guillard-Scope; p.83 Ribieras-Explorer; p.84 G. de Laubier; p.85 Sappa-C.E.D.R.I.; p.86 top Loirat-Explorer; bottom Sappa-C.E.D.R.I.; p.87 Sappa-C.E.D.R.I.; p.88 Sappa-C.E.D.R.I.; p.89 Martel-Top; p.90 S.Held; p.91 Bordas-Fotogram; p. 92 Burri-Magnum; p.93 top J.Bottin; bottom Loirat-Explorer; p.94 left Manos-Magnum; right Sioen-Cedri; p.95 Manos-Magnum; p.96 Errath-Explorer; p.96/7 J.Bottin; p.97 Manos-Magnum; p.98 Tuppin-Pix; p.99 F.Cornet; p.100 Boutin-Explorer; p.101 F.Cornet; p.102 Tuppin-Pix; p.103 top C.Lénars; bottom Bordas-Fotogram; p.104 top Levy-Cedri; bottom Levy-Cedri; p.105 R.McLeod; p.106 left Manos-Magnum; right Loirat-Explorer; p.107 Farantos-Photothèque S.D.P.; p.108 Boutin-Explorer; p.109 A.Rochegude; p.110 A.Rochegude; p.111 top A.Rochegude; bottom Monin-Top; p.112 S.Held; p.113 top Truchet-Fotogram; bottom Da Coasta-Pix; p.114 S.Held; p.115 S.Held; p.116 left F.Cornet; right Celiane-Fotogram; p.117 P.Lafond; p.118 Boyer-Explorer; p.119 top Rives-Cedri; bottom Pratt-Pries-Diaf; p.120 F.Cornet; p.121 Levy-Cedri; p.122 Putelat-Top; p.123 top Levy-Cedri; bottom Lessing-Magnum; p.124 Pratt-Pries-Diaf; p.125 top Févier-Top; bottom F.Cornet; p.126 left Beuzen-Explorer; right F.Cornet; p.127 J.-C. Chabrier; p.128 Freed-Magnum; p.129 J.Bottin; p.130 top E.Guillou; bottom Reichel-Top; p.131 Gould-Scope; p.132 Garnier-Photothèque S.D.P.; p.133 E.Guillou; p.134 top Arnaud-Pix; bottom Heitmann-Ana; p.135 Sioen-Cedri; p.136 top Durazzo-Ana; Durazzo-Ana;

p.137 Durazzo-Ana; p.138 Frey-Image Bank; p.139 Kohn-Cosmos; p.140 top Vergani-Image Bank; bottom M.Levassort; p.141 M.Levassort; p.142 M.Levassort; p.143 E.Guillou; p.144 Rochot-Atlas-Photo; p.145 top Durazzo-Ana; bottom Boulat-Cosmos; p.146 S.Marmounier; p.147 Bertinetti-Rapho; p.148 Luider-Rapho; p.149 M.Levassort; p.150 Ross-Rapho; p.151 left Kalvar-Magnum; right Brissaud-Rapho; p.152 top Durazzo-Ana; bottom Jovanne-Atlas-Photo; p.153 Yolka-Atlas-Photo; p.154 top Pertuisot-Pix; bottom Fischer-Pix; p.155 Pasquier-Rapho; p.156 P.Lafond; p.157 Fiore-Explorer; p.158 left P.Lafond; right Fiore-Explorer; p.159 Serval-Rapho; p.160 Desjardins-Top; p.161 P.Lafond; p.162 Pertuisot-Pix; p.163 Gabanou-Diaf; p.164 Desjardins-Top; p.165 J.-M. Steinlein; p.166 top M.Bruggmann; bottom M.Bruggmann; p.167 M.Bruggmann; p.168 Yolka-Atlas-Photo

Cover pictures
Top: Susan Griggs Agency
Bottom: Ted Spiegel